HOMOSEXUAL SECRET SOCIETIES

Cover picture: The All-Seeing Eye of God (Eye of Providence) tops a pyramid with thirteen steps (the original 13 American colonies) and is under the motto *Annuit Coeptis*, ''God approves our undertaking''. The Freemasons adopted the Eye in 1797, fourteen years after its American creation, meaning Freemasonry was not responsible for its conception, even if George Washington was a Freemason.

Revised 2020 Edition

1

My books include: *Cellini, Caravaggio, Cesare Borgia, Renaissance Murders, TROY, Greek Homosexuality, ARGO, Alcibiades the Schoolboy, RENT BOYS, Buckingham, Sailors and Homosexuality, The Essence of Being Gay, John (Jack) Nicholson, THE SACRED BAND, German Homosexuality, Gay Genius, SPARTA, Charles XII of Sweden, Mediterranean Homosexual Pleasure, CAPRI, Boarding School Homosexuality, VENICE, American Homosexual Giants, HUSTLERS* and *Christ has his John, I have my George: The History of British Homosexuality.* **I live in the South of France.**

CONTENTS
INTRODUCTION

INTRODUCTION

Homosexual societies have always been secret for the simple fact that one could lose one's head ... if lucky, lucky because the usual means was the far more painful burning at the stake. If beheading was found too soft, a miscreant's hands and feet could first be lopped off. Another highly popular method had a man hanged until nearly dead, then lowered and disemboweled before his very eyes, and finally beheaded and the body cut or torn into four pieces (drawn-and-quartered). He could also be castrated just before being gutted, and a popular variation, right up to this day, is having the castrated remains stuffed into his mouth, chocking him to death. Even when one escaped death, the consequences of boy-love were serious, the Oscar Wilde tragedy an example, and more men than one chose suicide over scandal, from the *richissime* Alfred Krupp (2) to General Hector MacDonald (7).

The only sanctuary that existed was boarding schools (1), boys literally locked in their dormitories at night, totally free to practice hard-core *Lord of the Flies* sexual acrobatics and fag-inspired masochism, an experience that certainly started out in pain for many, but for most it was the imperishable, never to be regained, always wistfully regretted time-of-their-lives, as only first love can be.

This book begins with the Templars for the simple reason that before Christianity smothered the world under a sheath of lead, obliging men into secrecy, one was intellectually free, and religious restrictions played no role in one's sexuality. Some enlightened lands escaped the damning forces of hypocrisy, Florence under the de' Medici for example, where even popes and cardinals had access to vagrant lads so numerous as to beggar the imagination of sultans and their boy harems.

A major section of the book concerns the Chaeronea Order, based on the Theban Sacred Band, the history of which will bring us full circle to that happier time where a Greek man and his boy could gain ultimate honor--before men and gods alike--by defending one another to the death.

THE TEMPLARS
1129 – 1312
Hospitalers – Hughes de Payens – Mamelukes – Philippe IV – Clement V – Great Schism – Guillaume de Nogaret – Jacque de Molay

The Templars was a quasi-secret society of valiant warriors: 6 out of 23 Templar Grand Masters died in battle or captivity and 20,000 Templars were killed Outremer, the Templar word for the Levant (the eastern Mediterranean). They were eventually put to death for homosexual practices, and what is indecipherable is how 230 of them were decapitated because they would not renounce their religious beliefs before their Muslim captors, yet later other Templars were accused of spitting on the cross and renouncing Christ.

A Templar

That the Templars (the Poor Fellow-Soldiers of Christ and of the Temple of Solomon) practiced homosexuality is certain, but perhaps the practice was no more extensive than in other groupings of men among themselves, in the absence of women, crucial solace if they were not to wither. That the Templars were exclusively homosexual is absurd, although, as in every society, exclusively homosexual Templar individuals existed. The Templars were misogynists, but all men were at the time. What took place seems to have been mostly between consenting adults as boys were not accepted, although lads from age 15 were. (In those times British boys were sent to serve in India at age 15, and at age 15 or 16 a European prince or king was expected to assure his lineage by producing sons. The Greeks considered boys of 15 the summit of sexual appeal, and were therefore

9

the domain reserved for the gods [although a supposed error in the translation of ancient works puts the real age of boy perfection at 16].) Whether the Templars in fact did spit on the cross and deny Christ is unknown. But it most probably did take place, and the explanation I've found was their refusal to accept idolatry, represented by both the cross and the deification of Jesus, certainly influenced by Islam which refuses to worship objects, and for whom Christ exists as a man, not a god. The very idea that a god could be produced by way of a woman's privates was, to Muslims, quite simply mad. Mad too, to Muslims, was trial by combat and judgment by ordeal (practiced by Templars), as well as medical treatments such as enemas and bleedings. Islam certainly also influenced the ease with which Templars turned to homosexuality, as Arabs--encouraged by the climate and scarcity of women--allowed sexual rapports of every nature.

The abbot Aelred de Rievaulx (1110 – 1167) declared that human love was less than the love of God, and married love was less than the love between males. Anselm, the Archbishop of Canterbury, wrote to a male friend: ''I do not doubt that we both love the other equally ... fused together in the fire of love ... suffer equally if our bodies are separated ... how great is our affection ... (we share) kiss for kiss, embrace for embrace.''

The Templars were sinners, but perhaps no more so than were other men then and now.

The Hospitalers existed at the time, but they were a group that cared for the spiritual and physical health of pilgrims in the Holy Land. For that reason the French noble Hugues de Payens went before the King of Jerusalem, Baldwin II, and the Patriarch, Warmund, for permission to mount a new monastic order that would protect the pilgrims against marauders, the geneses of the Templars. For this they were given a part of the Al-Aqsa Mosque on the Temple Mount, carefully allowing Moslems to enter and pray at the emplacement reserved for them. Templars were so poor they adopted as a symbol two knights riding a single horse, but by the time of their destruction they were so rich that kings fought over the spoils, and to this very day men search for their lost treasure as ardently as for the Holy Grail.

Two Templars shown riding on a single horse to symbolize their poverty.

Their recognition by the Council of Troyes in 1129, that freed them from the laws of men and the taxes of governments, along with their charter to protect the weak on the road to the holy shrines, brought in riches in the form of gold, land and castles that stretched from Ireland through France, Spain and Italy, to Outremer. Their wealth and their reputation for secure banking became such that pilgrims leaving, say, England for the Holy Land, placed their money with the Templars who gave them letters of credit, the first travelers' checks, cashed when they reached their destination, an enormous protection against piracy and other forms of thievery. They had their own fleet of ships and their own island, Cyprus, as well as the right to wear a white cloak and tunic, both adorned with a red cross. They were forced to have their hair cut short and to wear beards, and they vowed poverty, piety, obedience and chastity. $1/10^{th}$ of their food had to go to the poor and they were obliged to eat meat--limited to three times a week--to keep up their fighting strength. Like Muslims, should they die in battle they were assured a place in heaven, but without the Islamic 72 virgins that went with it. They were forbidden to leave the field as long as their flag was held high. As the first Christians were certain of the eminent destruction of the world, marriage was pointless. Cardinal Damian of Ostia wore an iron girdle around his loins, and regarded marriage as an excuse for sin. To make certain there would be no occasion for homosexual activity, Templars were to sleep in separate beds, dressed and wearing their boots. Dormitories were to be lit all night. Every moment of a Templar's life was regulated down to the way they could cut cheese, and every hour controlled, based on masses at Prime, Terce, Sext, None, etc.

Ponferrada, a stunning example of
Templar fortifications.

A unique characteristic concerning the
Templars was that they made a specialty of
accepting murderers and excommunicates
among their members. In fact, the assassins of
Thomas à Becket were sentenced to fourteen
years of service under the Templars.

Despite their efforts and those of Richard
I, Jerusalem was lost to Saladin in 1187 and
would remain under Islam until wrested from
the Turks in 1917 by the British.

The Templar flag.

The Templars were forced to retreat due to the Mamelukes, Slavic warriors captured from Albania to the steppes of Russia and raised as invulnerable fighters by their sultan masters whom they eventually overthrew. Led by the Muslim Baybars, and having no allegiance except to Allah, the Mamelukes took one Christian fortification after another, promising a safe retreat to those who surrendered, then massacred them all, except those they needed as slaves. They would move on to another castle that they surrounded with decapitated heads, promising to free the inhabitants if they gave up, gathering a new harvest of heads when they did. It was little wonder that the Christians were literally forced into the sea, and the Templars back to Cyprus. Later the Templars were thought to have been the first Freemasons, Freemasons who were excommunicated because they represented free thought while Catholicism could only grow through obscurantism based on mindless passivity, ignorance, gullibility and the threat of hell, the compost of most religions, but there is no real basis to the idea that the Templars had anything to do with Freemasonry.

In Europe the Templars still enjoyed tax-free luxury, beholding to none other than the pope and kings. One of the latter, Philippe IV of France, eyed Templar wealth that far exceeded his own. In fact, Philippe had borrowed astronomical sums from the Templars and he had an infallible way of erasing it all by simply erasing the Templars, the wealth of which, he planned, would go into his own purse. What he had in mind were the complaints of heresy lodged against the Templars, and although Philippe had already gone over the head of the pope, Benedict XIII, by imprisoning ecclesiastics, the uproar was such that he knew it would be better if he worked in tandem with a pope instead of against him in bringing the Templars to heel. And the moment was imminently propitious because for the last *eleven months* the Holy See had been empty, awaiting a decision from cardinals who couldn't decide on the right man. The least offensive was the Archbishop of Bordeaux, Bertrand de Got, a Frenchman, yet Bordeaux was under English rule and so he was a vassal of the English king Edward I, which made him the perfect choice for both England and France, both certain they could control his every move. Under the name of

Clement V, the new pope chose Avignon because at the time it was a site independent of France and Philippe IV. Clement did not rubber stamp everything Philippe wanted, but he did have an obsession: recovering Jerusalem, and Philippe--himself deeply and honestly religious--vowed to go there at the head of an army. *Two days* after receiving the papal tiara, Clement issued a bull proclaiming the new Crusade. Once liberated, the Levant would go to Philippe's brother Charles de Valois.

The origin of the above began when Philippe IV, called the Handsome (Philippe *le Bel*), wanted to tax church lands. Pope Boniface VIII disagreed, going so far as to excommunicate Philippe. *Le Bel* sent his henchman Guillaume de Nogaret and Italian mercenaries to waylay and capture Boniface whom they beat so severely he died a month after they released him. Boniface was succeeded by Benedict XI who, as stubborn as Boniface, died a year later, poisoned, said most, by Nogaret. Because of the stink raised by two papal murders, Philippe decided to buy cardinals in order for them to choose a French pope, the future Clement V, whom Philippe obliged to reside in Avignon (at the time technically the possession of the King of Sicily). Thus began the Great Schism, when Rome elected a pope of its own. Taking on the Templars after all of this was *pipi de chat* (dead easy) for someone of Philippe and Nogaret's determination, Nogaret who eventually died in his bed, his tongue ''horribly thrust out'', perhaps at Boniface.

The Templar treasure is reputed to consist of massive amounts of gold bullion, jewels, religious artifacts and explosive documents concerning the divinity of Christ. One possible place where it was buried has been explored for over 200 years, one expedition even financed by Franklin Roosevelt: the site is off the coast of Nova Scotia, on Oak Island.

A united front was needed, and Philippe convinced Clement to combine the Templars with the Hospitalers. The Temple Grand

Master, Jacques de Molay, completely illiterate as were most of the knights and the vast majority of the peoples of Europe, was against the unification because his group, founded on military exploits, had nothing to do with the Hospitalers, a charitable organization only. After all, the Knights Templar were the world's first and foremost Warrior Monks. Perhaps Molay was afraid the Hospitalers would give away all the wealth Templars had literally died to amass. Molay's refusal was the *casus belli* Philippe needed to crush the Templars and take their treasure.

15,000 Templars, says Piers Paul Read in his book *The Templars*, were rounded up in a single day, certainly impossible as that was the total number of Templars. Some sources state that less than 1,000 were ever questioned, of whom 60 were eventually executed. The leaders were imprisoned and some were tortured so severely by fire that their bones fell out of the skin. These confessed to spitting on the cross, to denying Christ, to indecent kissing on the mouth, buttocks and penis, and to homosexual acts, corruption and fraud. Those who were not tortured pleaded innocent to all charges. Most of those who had pleaded guilty under torture and were then promised they would not be further harmed if they told the truth, recanted. Those who recanted and were told they would be tortured again anyway, again pleaded guilty. When Molay opened his shirt to show his torture wounds to a group of visiting priests, they broke down and sobbed. Other Templars seem to have confessed to all or part of these acts during sincere confessions to their personal confessors. Some maintained that when they entered a monastery they were told outright they could have sex with other members, especially as Christ had had his John. Sexual relations were declared to not be sinful, and the climate within the monasteries was such that they took place naturally.

In order of severity (least severe to most severe), homosexual crimes were solitary masturbation, mutual masturbation, sex between the legs (intercrural) and anal sex. The most stringent sentences involved spiritual fathers--Templar officials--who had their way on their spiritual sons, the new, young recruits. The Grand Master of Cyprus was accused by one lad of abusing him three times in one night.

The Templars who repented were welcomed back into the church and dispersed separately to various monasteries, many crippled for life due to torture. Two men had stepped forward to defend the Templar leaders in courts of law. After losing their cases both dropped off the surface of the earth, presumably murdered.

In Spain the Templars had fought against the Moors, fueling the anger of Saladin. The Templars had fed 26,000 Spaniards during a famine, and they had come to the aid of Barcelona when threatened by the French. In thanks, the Spanish king James II seized their entire holdings.

In the end Clement decreed that Templar wealth, land, castles and houses would go to the Hospitalers. Philippe IV, Edward II of England and James II of Spain agreed, after taking what they could for themselves. Only in Cyprus did all the Templar fortune go to the Hospitalers.

In 1312 Philippe and his three sons, and Edward II of England, took up the Crusaders' cross as promised. The four top Templar leaders, among them Jacques de Molay, were sentenced to life imprisonment, but Molay and one other retracted their confessions when they learned of the harsh sentence. His last request was to face the cathedral of Notre

Dame, and that his hands be freed so he could pray, both supplications granted. He and his fellow Templar went up in flames on the Ile-des-Javiaux in the Seine, Molay summoning both Philippe and Clement to appear before God and His punishment within a year. Both did exactly that.

Martyrdom on the Ile-des-Javiaux in the Seine.

On the Ile-des-Javiaux the bones and ashes of the martyrs were collected as saintly relics.

Memorial to Molay facing Ile de la Cité.

FREEMASONS
1300s
Oscar Wilde – Frederick the Great - Cecile Rhodes - Horatio Kitchener - Richard Burton

Freemasonry sprang from fraternal groupings of stone workers somewhere in the 1300s. The basic unite is the Lodge, each Lodge being independent of others, with no centralized control or even surveillance. Freemasonry members work their way through degrees of Freemasonry, from Entered Apprentice to Fellow Craft to the ultimate, Master Mason. Masonry meetings are said to be highly ritualized, and of supreme importance to Masons is their obligation to contribute to charities, to education and to disaster relief. Men are never invited to join a Lodge (the first founded in London in 1717), but those who request to do so on their own initiative must be introduced to other members by a Lodge fellow who knows the candidate well enough to recommend him. These introductions take place at informal Lodge social gatherings. Most candidates are mature adults.

Strangely (for me) is the fact that most Lodges demand that members believe in a supreme being, and in Sweden only Christians are accepted. The Grand Orient de France, founded in 1773, accepts atheists, a point of discord with other Lodges (although, paradoxically, discussions of both politics and religion are forbidden within the Lodges). Worldwide, there are perhaps 6,000,000 Freemasons.

Pope Clement VII was first to decry the Masons for their minimal demand that one need only believe in a deity, and in 1917 those becoming Freemasons were automatically excommunicated, a law rescinded in 1983 (rescinded in the sense that reference to Freemasons was dropped). Protestant objections to Masons seems centered on

Masonic mysticism, occultism and, some maintain, Satanism. Masonic ideology displeased the Nazis as well, and perhaps 200,000 Masons were destroyed by Hitler's miscreants.

There are probably as many homosexuals among Masons as there are in the population at large, but they nonetheless had the most notorious member of them all, Oscar Wilde.

Oscar Wilde

Born in Dublin, Wilde's father had been a Freemason and thanks to Prince Leopold, Queen Victoria's sixth son, Oscar was accepted into the Apollo University Lodge of which Leopold was the Worshipful Master. Others maintain that it was his friend John Bodley who took Wilde to his first Masonry event, where he found the boys, said Bodley, ''gorgeous''. The connection between Apollo, the Masons and homosexuality becomes clear thanks to this extract from my book *SPARTA*:

Although boys can't be counted on to tell the exact truth about their first loves, Apollo claims that it was the beauty of Hyacinth that lured him into night games at the side of lads. Now, Hyacinth was a Spartan, born during the Mycenaean period, long before the laws of Lycurgus came into effect, making life in Sparta more difficult. After Lycurgus, boys were raised in the women's quarters until age seven, after which they were put in barracks and formed groups called herds ruled over by an older boy known as the boy-herder, who wielded a whip. They slept on reed beds, wore red cloaks, ate a sickening broth and were taught to forage for food because there was never enough in their communal messes. From age twelve the boys were free to choose older friends with whom they formed a sexual bond, friends who taught them what they needed to know about warfare and loyalty to the Spartan state. But when Hyacinth was born--before the laws of Lycurgus--Sparta was a city much like all the others in Greece, much like Athens, where boys Hyacinth's age could get a full education, had plenty to eat, and were free to hang out around perfume and oil shops, and visit the barber to have their hair cared for and, when older, their nascent beards modishly trimmed.

Apollo would at times leave the stress of giving oracles at Delphi to sprawl out in the meadows of grass and flowers next to the Spartan river Eurotas. At the time Delphi was the most important site in Greece, just after Mount Olympus itself. Delphi. In the beginning the gods freed two high-flying eagles, one from the East, the other from the West. They met on the lofty crags of a great mountain that loomed over a jagged valley and the far-off port of Cirrha. Here was the sacred center of the universe; here was the spiritual navel of the Hellenes; here was Delphi, home of Apollo.

For Apollo had left his birthplace on Cycladic Delos to teach Man wisdom by revealing to him the future. Apollo traveled to the heights of Mount Parnassus where he destroyed the snake-like dragon, Python, its guardian. Then, with the help of the Muses and the consent of Mother Earth, he recruited sailors from a passing Cretan ship whom he made priests, and irreproachable villagers from the nearby village of Krissa whom he ordained priestesses, sometimes called Pythonesses in memory of the dragon. He built a temple, initiated the love of the arts, taught moderation and humaneness in all things, and himself tried to exemplify the virtuous life.

But as any lad knows, at times a boy needs more than moderation and virtue. At times he wants to let out all the stops. That's why Apollo chose the meadows around Eurotas. He loved clear streams and to bask in the sun and watch the Spartan boys, naked as the day, come down to swim and horse around. It made Apollo smile to see lads as frisky as yearlings, without a care in the world, while he had to continually divvy up oracles about which king was legitimate and which was not, which state would win a war if it crossed a certain river; and what the future held in store for this lass and her beau, or for that king and his kingdom, not to mention his obligation to adjudicate over poisonings, incest, murders and crucifixions. In a sense, the least of his worries was the wear and tear between his dad Zeus and ma Hera, and his brothers and sisters always and ever quarrelling.

The boy the others called Hyacinth was clearly better looking than the rest and better built, so unlike Apollo who was a bit hunky around the waist and whose buttocks were a shade large for a man. Hyacinth's were small, round and looked as solid as white marble. Of course, the sun, Apollo's brother Helios, had shaded the boy a tawny brown. The lad had long hair like Apollo, although the lad's fell over his shoulders, while Apollo's was sort of bunched up in a bun over his neck. Hyacinth and Apollo met when Hyacinth went to retrieve a discus he and his friends were throwing back and forth. Hyacinth was surprised to nearly stumble over Apollo, hidden in the high grass, but the god of Light had a nice warm smile and an easy way he'd learned over centuries on Earth, being Immortal and all. They fell into conversation and when his friends went home for dinner Hyacinth preferred to remain and talk with this man whose knowledge was greater than anyone the boy had ever known. Hyacinth soon left because he too was hungry but he returned day after day, his quest for knowledge insatiable. Apollo told stories about kingdoms the boy had never even heard of, and tales about kings and queens and battles and great warriors. They did physical exercises together and soon Apollo was in better shape than at any time in his life.

When Hyacinth and his friends did athletics they infibulated themselves. It was considered obscene to expose the penis glans, so a precaution was to tie up the end of the foreskin with a string that was attached to the base of the penis at the bush. Unlike our days, a long penis was apparently considered unseemly. Infibulation corrected this problem too. Some of the boys had the string from the foreskin attached to a string they wore around their waists, a method that stretched the penis upwards and fully exposed the balls, of which they were proud. The string was called the *kynodesmē*, the leash for the dog.

Lying with boys was normal intimacy for Hyacinth as the girls in Sparta were forced to remain locked up in their parent's homes and boys just naturally fell to giving each other a hand, and other things in preparation for later marriages. Hyacinth was especially attracted to Apollo because the god seemed to combine both sexes. His hips nearly resembled those of women and his breasts were much fuller than a Spartan boy's. In Sparta the lads were all slim-waisted and their pectorals were squared off and as hard as rock. So what happened was more of a surprise to Apollo than to the boy. They had met and now they loved, a new kind of experience for the otherwise very experienced god. In Greek and later Roman love, the man was always the penetrator. That much was clear. But Apollo being Apollo, the swordsman may have been, exceptionally, the young Hyacinth. At any rate, the god of Light was thrilled. Here was someone he could train with, run with, talk with, laugh with, a boy who introduced him to his friends, an intimacy that remained closed between the two of them, but was hugely enlarged into a social event in which Apollo, Hyacinth and their friends were soon all laughing and playing and swimming and exchanging stories and knowledge. And Apollo loved the boys' laughter, so free and uninhibited and carefree and unbridled. While he and Hyacinth gave their youthful bodies in uncomplicated love, around them, hidden in the folds of grass, the other boys did the same, in pairs and in groups. Unrestrained, unruly, totally gratuitous, the end being a liberation of the demanding forces their bodies imposed on them since puberty, and then a race to the river to wash off. Hyacinth never pressured Apollo for something in exchange for the pleasure Apollo accorded him, because their release was mutual and thoroughly fulfilling and totally disinterested. Nor did the boy ever just lie there waiting for something to happen; theirs were two active virilities with never a second of monotony or boredom, something the god had not experienced with a mortal girl.

And then Apollo lost what was the most precious being to ever grace his long, long existence. Apollo had been used to inflicting pain, as the time he'd skinned alive the mortal Marsyas when in a musical contest the poor earthling--claiming to be the better musician than Apollo--was outsmarted by the god who could play his lyre rightside-up or upside-down, while Marsyas could only make music through one end of his flute. Apollo and his fellow gods were used to raising those around them to incredible heights, before destroying them utterly, as they did Croesus, making him rich and powerful beyond dreams. Then he lost his empire to Cyrus and his precious son was gored by a boar. Now it was the god's turn to suffer.

He and his precious belovèd had spent the morning mountain climbing, they'd swum and exercised, and were now throwing the discus, their bodies, Ovid tells us, were naked and sleek with oil, while their friends, stretched out in the high grass, were chatting as boys do, and applauding the god and the youth. Now, the West Wind had been spying on the couple and had decided that he too would try his hand at boy-love. But when Hyacinth paid him no attention, he became insanely jealous and caused the discus, thrown by Apollo, to fall to the ground where it rebounded and struck the forehead of the sweet youth. Hyacinth fell and where his blood fecundated the earth a bed of hyacinth, rose-red flowers, sprang up. Apollo wailed the loss of his belovèd, arousing Zeus from his noonday sleep. He saw the beauty of the boy entwined in Apollo's arms, as the god of Light shed tears that marked the flowers with spots of white, and like a flower too the boy's head hung lifeless as though cut off at the stem. Thusly were Zeus's eyes opened to the wonder of the love of boys. He immediately took a wise decision: he too would find a companion to while away his days in mutual contentment, his nights in shared bliss, but as a first step, he would make the lad immortal.

He thusly abducted the Trojan youth Ganymede for his bed and--to ward off smirks--dissimulated the fact by making him his cupbearer.

Soon Man followed suit. The Spartans made boy-love a virile pursuit in which lovers became valorous warriors, preferring death to the betrayal of their loved ones. The Athenians turned boy-love into a philosophical pastime in which, thanks to

Eros, the intellectual and the physical were joined to make a new, self-sufficient man. In time the Trojan Aeneas would take the custom to the city he was destined to found on the banks of the Tiber. But this would be neither the virile nor intellectual fusion of body and soul known to the Greeks, but a monstrous, degenerative debauch of painted faces, effeminate bodies and fat slavering perverts.

Apollo had put all his science into reviving Hyacinth's still-warm body but its life had flitted away and already Hades had risen from the Underworld to claim what was his. Apollo stopped him with a glance, and womanish or not, Hades knew the look in those eyes and trembled, for he was confronted with the god of Light himself, who, next to Hermes, was Zeus's favorite son. So he crept back into the caverns of molten slime that awaited him. Apollo gently picked up the boy and carried him to the Elysian Fields, meadows and islands untouched by sorrow, a blessed land, the home of heroes and the deathless gods, a land free from toil, cradle of perpetual springs and shady groves and bubbling brooks, a cornucopia warmed by its own sun and illumined by its own stars--and eternally cooled by the West Wind, an obligation demanded by Apollo under pain of death.

And there Hyacinth lives, in Elysium, and in us, for the blood he shed nourished the sweet earth, the sweet earth that nourishes us so abundantly to this very day.

End of extract and back to Wilde:

His four years as a Mason took place during his studies at Magdalene College, Oxford. As I've written on other occasions in this book, homosexuality in the Masons is most probably on a par with homosexuality elsewhere in our society, but there are periods in history when homosexuality becomes nearly a fad, as Duncan Grant stated when he wrote that during the years of the Bloomsbury Set (8), and during the time of the early Apostles, even heterosexuals claimed to have male lovers in order to be in vogue. Albert Pike lived around then and many historians refer to his works. Pike (1809-1891) ascended to the highest degree of Masonry, the 33rd, was a Scot whose *magnum opus* was the *Morals and Dogma of the Ancient and Accepted Scottish Rite of Freemasonry.* According to Pike secrecy is the foundation of Masonry: Masonry ''conceals its secrets from all except the Adepts and Sages, or the Elect, and uses false explanations and misinterpretations of its symbols to mislead those who deserve only to be misled; to conceal the Truth, which it calls Light, from them, and to draw them away from it. Truth is not for those who are unworthy or unable to receive it, or would pervert it. The symbols and ceremonies of Masonry have more than one meaning. They rather *conceal* than *disclose* the Truth. They hint it only.''

As for homosexuals, some historians interpret the following as meaning that the Masons practice oral sex: An initiate ''commemorates in sacramental observance this mysterious passion; and while partaking of the raw flesh of the victim, seems to be invigorated by a fresh draught from the fountain of universal life.... Hence the significance of the phallus'' (9). Pike goes on, according to some, to say that members engage in orgies: ''He mingles with the crowd of Initiates, and, crowned with flowers, celebrates with them the holy orgies.'' From Pike's writings it becomes clear that Freemasonry is an all-male secret society based on the inherent superiority of men in every domain a man puts his mind to conquer, even *haute couture* and *haute cuisine*, a superiority so vast and all-inclusive that a Mason wouldn't even stoop to compare himself to the other sex. Sharing that superiority among themselves is the very *raison d'être* of their existence as brethren.

The whole of Wilde's existence, like that of Byron, was bigger than life. Born rich, surrounded by servants, a German governess and French maid, physically he was not one of the boys that other boys--deadly serious about their sex--fought over, boys they possessed at night until the next beautiful face came along. Wilde's personality became flippant, as a way of compensating for his lack of looks, his big, awkward body too padded to be erotically attractive, too ungainly, a face too homely. He therefore overcompensated, as do actors: jackets with large checkers, bright ties, high collars, huge hats tilted over one or the other ear. Joseph Pearce in his *The Unmasking of Oscar Wilde*, 2000, calls his transformation into a dandy the emergence from a kind of ''chrysalis'', and it was exactly that. He was said to have been physically capable of taking care of himself should anyone mock his style, and intellectually he knew his classics and his philosophers, from Plato to Spencer.

Everything about Wilde was exaggerated.

Wilde at first toyed with heterosexuality. A marriage produced two sons, Cyril and Vyvyan, whose last names were changed to Holland after the scandal. Both were educated in Switzerland. Cyril became an army captain and served in India before being killed by a sniper in W.W.I. Wilde's son Vyvyan served in both World Wars and died at age 80. Both sons were prevented by law from ever seeing their father again, although Vyvyan accompanied his father's remains to his last resting place, at the side of Wilde's last lovers, Douglas and Ross.

In 1886 he met 17-year-old Robert Ross who, enamored of his poetry, seduced his hero, Wilde, age 32. Ross claims to have been Wilde's first homosexual experience, an impossibility given boarding-school rampant sexuality and Wilde's trips to Italy, for all time an English and German sporting grounds, and rightly so, as Italian boys are sexually precocious, unbridled, and among the most beautiful in the world. After Ross the floodgates opened, and even Wilde's bookseller could hardly keep up with the homosexual literature Wilde was forced to pay dearly for.

Robbie Ross, age 24 in this picture, remained Wilde's loyal friend until Wilde's death, aiding him financially. He became Wilde's legal executor and made sure that Wilde's two boys received the royalties from his books. Openly gay, Ross was a journalist and art critic. He had had sexual relations with a boy of 16 who admitted to sleeping with

Lord Alfred Douglas in Ross's home, but the boy's parents, to avoid scandal, did not press charges. He died in 1918. In 2008 the University of Bradford named its library collection the Robbie Ross Liberation Library.

Richard Le Gallienne followed in 1888, seduced too by Wilde's poetry but he soon became disinterested in Wilde himself.

Author and poet, Le Gallienne lived in Menton France.

In 1889 he met John Gray, 23, the lad who became his *Dorian Gray*. At the time it was extraordinary for a poor boy to work himself into the upper-classes, something

Gray did, starting out as a carpenter at age 18, learning French, German and Latin on his own, succeeding in Civil Service examinations which opened the ranks of government employment, and then his meeting with Wilde and their sexual union. *The Portrait of Dorian Gray* came out in 1890. In the book Gray goes on to ever-mounting perversion, as did Wilde, and, later, from prison Wilde wrote Douglas that he should have been wise enough to remain with Gray or someone like him. Amusingly, W.H. Smith refused to sell *The Portrait of Dorian Gray*, calling it filth.

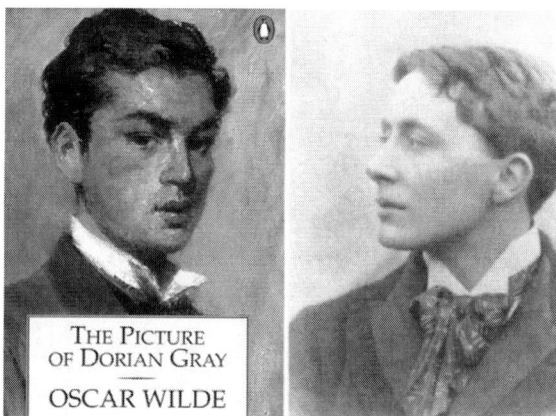

Gray became a poet and a priest, and died four months after the death of his friend, mentor and life partner Marc-André Raffalovich, a poet and writer on homosexuality, with whom his relations were said to have been chaste.

It was assuredly difficult to bear Wilde's cynicism, arrogance, flippancy, posturing decadence and his need for upper-class luxury. As he himself wrote, ''I am not really myself except in the midst of elegant crowds, in the heart of rich districts or amid sumptuous ornamentation or palace hotels, [waited on] by an army of servants, the warm caress of plush carpet under my feet''. Hints of Wilde's ''Socratism'', a veiled allusion to his homosexuality, circulated after *Dorian Gray*, perhaps part of the reason he became a society darling, increasingly invited out by increasingly better-classed people. A dinner dandy, an underworld denizen at night, an habitué of the fleshpots, nothing particularly extraordinary, then as now. He met 18-year-old Beardsley who illustrated Wilde's *Salomé*, Wilde's need for cock as all-consuming as only Beardsley could depict it.

Lysistrata: Adoration of the Penis.

18-year-old Beardsley (Aubrey, 1872-1898) was retained by Wilde to illustrate his works, especially Wilde's *Salomé* when Beardsley was 20; he was one of the few to remain faithful to the playwright to the end of his life. Beardsley was known for his Art-Nouveau illustrations in black ink. He had traveled to Paris where the influences of Toulouse-Lautrec and the Parisian passion for Japanese prints changed the artistic direction of his life. He stated that his own ambition was the grotesque. He dressed as a Wilde-like dandy, and sexually could have been anything from asexual to insistent rumors that he impregnated his sister. He converted to Roman Catholicism as did Wilde, and requested that his obscene drawings be destroyed--they weren't.

Suffering from tuberculosis, he withdrew to Menton in France (my own second hometown), as had Le Gallienne, where he died at age 25.

After *Salomé* Wilde wrote *Lady Windermere's Fan*, a play among many that will assure his celestial immortality (of which he himself was certain).

He came across the faultless beauty of Douglas in 1890, a budding poet at Oxford, whom Wilde was said to have worshipped. Both liked teenage male prostitutes, and both had the means to assuage their desires. Their degeneracy was total, but degeneracy is what very man wishes for himself sometime in his life. They were involved in the Cleveland Street Telegram Scandal, detailed elsewhere, and were open to blackmail. Both Douglas and Wilde played Douglas's mother and father for fools because neither guessed what was going on, as parents do not generally raise their boys to be sodomised, especially not by flabby, faded lechers like Wilde.

Douglas, nicknamed Bosie (Lord Alfred Bruce, 9th Marquess of Queensberry, 1970-1945), is a highly unpleasant personage described as spoiled and arrogant, who ran roughshod over Wilde, both outdoing each other in lechery. Reckless, he gave his old clothes to his male rent boys (10), forgetting to remove letters between him and Wilde, obliged thereafter to pay out blackmail. His father, the 8th Marquess of Queensberry, wrote a letter to him calling him a ''miserable creature'' whose mother he had divorced in order to not ''run the risk of bringing more creatures in the world like yourself.'' Douglas's brother was killed in a hunting accident, under strange circumstances, after rumors began circulating that he was having a homosexual affair with the then Prime

Minister, Lord Rosebery. It was Douglas who coined the phrase, the love that dare not speak its name.

In the meantime his plays, *Salomé* and *Fan,* were presented to sell-out crowds, the horseshit piled up in front of the theaters proof of the numerous carriages that pulled up to the entrance. (The reason why, in France, one wishes an actor luck by crying out *Merde*! [Shit!], which hailed back to the times that a huge quantity meant a huge success.) *An Ideal Husband* followed, followed by *A Woman of No Importance*, and Douglas made a point of being seen with Wilde during each first presentation. *The Importance of being Ernest* came out in 1894 and Wilde and Douglas went to Algeria where they met up with André Gide and the unlimited number of Arab boys all three were there to enjoy. Douglas was then 24, Wilde 40.

In 1895 Douglas's father the Marquess of Queensbury left a card at Wilde's residence addressed ''To Oscar Wilde, ponce and somdomite,'' misspelling the word in his fury. Wilde had the Marquess arrested and charged with criminal libel. Frank Harris, the famous author of the highly pornographic *My Life and*

Loves, and Bernard Shaw, told him that if he didn't drop the proceedings he would be destroyed. Wilde, the now most famous playwright in England, was too disdainful to heed the supplications. He would pay with his life, for from then onwards an early death was the direction his destiny took.

During his trial the Marquess said he lived for one reason, to save his son. And it may have been the truth. The boys called on to testify to Wilde being a sodomite were so numerous that when the Marquess was pronounced innocent the court irrupted in applause. Wilde himself was immediately incarcerated. Wilde's trial brought more witnesses against him, one who maintained ''He told me to come into his bedroom and worked me up with his hand and made me spend in his mouth.'' Hotel staff commented on the boys in his bed, the fecal stains and vaseline-stiff sheets, resulting in Wilde being sentenced to two years of hard labor.

Once released from jail Wilde returned to Douglas, thereby costing Wilde his wife and two sons forever (this being the last straw for her). Wilde and Douglas met in Naples but the truism that one cannot return, again justified itself. The boy had lost his freshness and

Wilde was visibly old. They rapidly separated, leaving Wilde nothing more than himself.

He went to Paris, the greatest city in the world when one is young, as I well know having spent a third of my life there. But Wilde was penniless and haggard. It was then he said, ''The cruelty of a prison sentence starts when you come out.''

Douglas did attend Wilde's funeral-- Wilde dead at age 46--during which Douglas had a heated public argument with another of Wilde's former lovers, Robert Ross, who had been with Wilde to the very end in Paris, and blamed Douglas for not having done enough to keep Wilde out of dire poverty. Douglas married and had a son who spent most of his life in an asylum for the mentally disturbed. Douglas spent six months in jail for falsely accusing Churchill of lying during the war, where he wrote his *In Excelsis*, as Wilde had written his *De Profundis* in prison. He died at age 74 and was interred alongside his mother, both under a single stone. Two people attended his funeral.

The Marquess of Queensberry died in 1900, requesting to be cremated and that ''no Christian tomfooleries'' were to be performed, my own wish exactly. He left £20,000 to his son Douglas, a part of which Wilde had requested Douglas turn over to him, stating that he deserved it. Douglas disagreed. Wilde died in the same year as the Marquess. He maintained that he had lived and died for love, which, in our imperfect world, could mean fecal-stained and vaseline-stiff sheets.

Frederick the Great
1712 - 1786

Napoleon felt that Frederick was the greatest tactical genius of all time, the reason for his proclaiming, standing above Frederick's grave, ''Gentlemen, if this man were still alive I would not be here.''

Frederick's grave marker.

Frederick, a Freemason, said that the key to his success was foresight, the ability to see the evolution of events in advance. This was followed by the audacity of the attack, destroying the enemy from an unexpected direction, all of which implied, as he further said himself, donning the skins of a lion and a fox. The Seven Years' War made the Prussian reputation as the world's greatest fighting power, one it has to this very day. It was the reason why General Washington bent over backwards to assure himself of the services of von Steuben, the Prussian who had not only been taught by Frederick, but had been Frederick's aide-de-camp (2). In the Battle of Rossbach Frederick defeated a combined force of French and Austrian troops, 41,000 men, with his own army of 21,000, leaving the field strewn with 10,000 dead to his losses of 550. At the Battle of Leuthen he confronted

80,000 Austrians with his army of 36,000, killing 7,000 and taking 20,000 prisoners. With every battle he risked everything, his army, his kingdom and his life, and he very nearly lost it all more than once. He maintained that wars had to be short if one didn't want the population to be decimated, resources depleted and army discipline weakened.

Frederick the Great by Anton Graff.

Civil wars are horrors, at times pitting fathers against sons, and what happened between Frederick William and his son Frederick could easily have ended in Frederick William's murdering his boy in one of the rages that characterized him, just as Ivan the Terrible had cut the throat of his son when mad with anger, and Peter the Great had murdered his boy (11). Frederick William once beat Frederick so severely that he told him if his own father had gone so far he would have killed himself in shame, while Frederick took the trouncing like a lowly serf. Such disrespect from a father was endlessly fueled by Frederick himself trying to be too clever, outwardly showing respect while in reality scoffing at Frederick William who knew exactly what the boy was up to. Frederick William, despite his boorish vulgarity, had worked himself to the bone to make Prussia into a veritable powerhouse that he naturally wanted continued by his son. Yet Frederick showed no sign of sharing any of his father's qualities. He was messy, unkempt, he preferred poetry, books and the company of his mother and sister to his father's banquets between men only, and he couldn't even ride a horse without falling off. A boy his father couldn't figure out, and once admitted he would give anything to be able to open his skull to see what was going on in the lad's brain.

The mystery is how Frederick turned out to be one of the world's greatest strategists, going infinitely farther than his father, even if, as we shall see, luck often played an uncannily important part in his successes.

Frederick decided to flee to England accompanied by his lover Hans Hermann von Katte. Both were rounded up, along with other officers, and imprisoned. Frederick was given a questionnaire by his father, the key question asking him if he deserved to be king after dishonoring himself by deserting his regiment, and if not, would he therefore renounce his right to the throne in order that his life be spared? Frederick answered that the king would decide if he were to live or die, but although his life did not mean all that much to him, the king would certainly not be so merciless.

Historians nearly unanimously believe that Frederick William was more than capable of putting his son to death, and while waiting to decide he ordered that Frederick be obliged to watch the execution of von Katte, whose head was severed from his body. Von Katte had written to his father, begging him to forgive him for the sorrow he would cause, forgive him for dashing all the hopes his father had had for him, aware that he would not be a comfort in his father's old age, sad that he would die in the spring of his youth, without fulfilling the future his father had so carefully planned for him. Katte also wrote to Frederick William promising to be the most loyal of his officers and begging for clemency, receiving no response. One wonders if Frederick William knew about the love between Katte and his son. As for the others caught up in the tragedy, they were jailed until Frederick became king and freed them all.

von Katte

Of course, we can never know the inner workings of the mind, the reasons for our motivations, the reality that one can grow up a choir boy and mute into a butcher of men. We would like to make Shakespearean windows into one's soul, as Frederick William wished in order to understand the workings of his son Frederick. So following the shock of seeing his lover's decapitation Frederick's reaction was so strange, and the reasons for it so lost in the convolutions of his brain, that the truth will never be known. Had he not become great the story would end here. We would not go on to relate how he fell to his knees before the tyrant who had sired him, kissing the boots of the monster who had taken the young life of his lover. But he did become great, and so the story will continue, one perplexing to the writer and the reader. Real or chameleon-like, Frederick became a model student, applying himself to the mastery of affairs, taking over a troop of boys his father accorded him, tirelessly drilling and exercising them, a troop soon to be enlarged to an army when Frederick William accorded more responsibility. Freed from prison, he was allowed to take part in the administration of the town where he was held captive, Küstren, where he learned the fundamentals of bureaucracy. He was even given a wife, a woman who would adore him until her last breath, like a dog boundlessly in love with the master that kicked it way, love as mindless as that which Frederick outwardly showered on his father. Frederick later said he had ''honored'' her, French--his preferred language--for fucking (as there was certainly no *love* involved), and it may have been so, at least *once*. From then on he found satisfaction with men as brilliant as Algarotti (2) or as simple as his boy aides-de-camp, but here the mystery is so complete that we run the spectrum of those who believe he had a new recruit every night, to those who maintain that he had somehow been injured when mercury was injected into his genitals as a way of curing syphilis, so mutilated that he could never function sexually again. One of his closest, most intimate friends was Voltaire, *the* personification of the Enlightenment, whom some believe was intimate with Frederick, but who, after falling out with the king, wrote a book listing Frederick's loves, proof that he was in no way impotent--if what Voltaire wrote was true.

Of course, the inconceivable trauma of seeing his lover decapitated, and the near certainty of his own imminent death, may have changed Frederick, or, as Christopher

Clark in his wonderful *Iron Kingdom* (2006) so perfectly put it: ''Did the events of 1730 forge a new artificial persona ... locked within the nautilus hull of a convoluted nature? Or did they merely deepen and confirm a tendency towards self-concealment and dissimulation that was already well developed in the adolescent prince? The question is ultimately unanswerable.''

When war between Britain and France broke out in 1754 Frederic saw his chance at both expansion and to strike against Saxony, an aggressive threat on his borders, by simply seizing the country.

Saxony circled, seized by Frederick in 1756.

This set off a chain reaction of alliances: Austria joined forces with France in hopes of regaining Silesia, Britain joined forces with Prussia against France, and Russia aligned with Austria against Prussian expansion until one of history's greatest and most unexpected *coups de théâtre* took place--another proof of Frederick's incredible luck: Tsar Peter III came to the throne and joined forces with Frederick whom the Russian boy-king worshipped.

During the war Frederick won some battles so impressively that it's extremely hazardous to guess how he did it: at the Battle of Rossbach for example his 20,000 Prussians came up against 40,000 French, and when the firing ended 10,000 French bodies were strewn over the battlefield to 500 Prussian losses.

On the other hand the new Holy Roman Empress, Maria Theresa, had had her troops trained in Prussian tactics, so when Frederick tried his signatory oblique attack the Austrians were ready, leaving 14,000 dead Prussians to nurture the sol of Kolin, against 8,000 Austrian lads.

Frederick won against Russia during the Battle of Zorndorf, but lost 13,000 men to

Russia's 18,000. That Russia, by far Frederick's most deadly foe, then withdrew, thanks to Peter, was a colossal miracle. Then Catherine the Great had her husband Peter III murdered, but she did not reenter the conflict--still more dumb luck for Frederick. That said, no other army at the time was as cruel as the Russians, for whom simply maiming was not an alternative to cutting off noses and ears before disemboweling men, women and children, and neither sex--men nor women--had to necessarily be alive to undergo the bestiality of sexual assaults. By the end of the Seven Years' War 400,000 Prussians had lost their lives.

The disappearance of Poland in 1795, a country bigger than France, is the most incredible incongruity in history. A first partition took place between Frederick's Prussia and Catherine's Russia in 1772. For Frederick the act of joining western Prussia to eastern Prussia, creating the all-powerful entity seen in the map below, was the immense triumph of his reign. Long before the reality of the partition he had recognized Poland as being the sick man of Europe, and compared the country to an artichoke that he would devour one leaf at a time. Poland had an elected monarchy that anyone from any nation could hold: homosexual Henry III (5) became its monarch thanks to the tireless efforts and monies of his mother, the inimitable Catherine de' Medici, and Catherine the Great herself had placed her lover Poniatowsky on the country's throne as a way of directing its every move and of freeing her bedroom for the young soldiers she spotted from the windows of her palace, healthy males whose warmth she herself claimed she needed every single day.

The result of an elective monarchy and a vague constitution led to anarchy outside of Poland's borders (anarchy between states that quarreled over who would possess her) and civil disturbances within, anarchy the invaders used as an excuse for ''saving'' the country by biting off chunks of it, the largest for Russia, 13%, the next largest for Austria, 12%, and what was needed by Frederick to unite Brandenburg to the Duchy of Prussia, 5%.

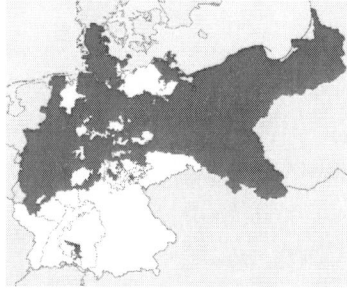

Kingdom of Prussia at its greatest.

Frederick had a unique and quasi-absolute respect for freedom of expression, allowing it in the press and even permitting the circulation of Voltaire's book entailing his homosexual encounters. He fought for the rights of the common man, the most sensational case, one that had the citizenry on the edge of their seats, was the trial against a miller, Arnold, who refused to pay his noble landlord rent when said landlord cut off the supply of water to Arnold's mill, diverting it into fish ponds for the noble's own use. Three courts found Arnold guilty, infuriating Frederick to the point that he had the third verdict's judges jailed for a year. The next trial found Arnold innocent and he was reimbursed for the totality of his losses.

In another intercession into the justice of his country, Frederick personally intervened in the case of a peasant who had penetrated his donkey sexually, stating that a man had the right to put his penis wherever he wished. He welcomed Julien Offray de la Mettrie to his court, the author of the *Art of Orgasm* and the *Little Guy with the Big Cock*. Baculard d'Arnaud, another friend, penned *The Art of Fucking* and Frederick was said to have written erotic prose lost to us. An unknown source published that Frederick fucked stable boys, pages, recruits and whoever else came his way during the day. Voltaire who knew his intimate side better than any source outside Frederick's court wrote that Frederick enjoyed a boy as soon as he rose in the morning, a lackey or a cadet, adding that it was Frederick the bottom.

La Mettrie's unbridled sexuality was expressed in his book *Discours sur le bonheur*, an appeal to hedonistic pleasure that was said to have shocked Voltaire and Diderot, men *pourtant* known for their unbridled libertinage. La Mettrie was a doctor, and in addition to his no-holds-barred erotic palaver with Frederick he was used as a court physician. He is said to have died of indigestion following a meal in which he downed a platter of *pâté de faisan aux truffes.*

We'll leave Frederick the Great here, but his whole story can be found in my book *Prussian Homosexuality*.

Cecil Rhodes

Cecil Rhodes, one of many monumental Freemasons, is singled out here because he was also homosexual. A whole country, Rhodesia, was named for him (now Zimbabwe and Zambia) and his immense wealth helped build Cape Town where he was Prime Minister and funded today's Rhodes Scholarship. English born, he was sent to South Africa at age 17 to improve his health. He was trading in diamonds at age 18 and in 1888 he founded De Beers diamond company, named after a farmer on whose land he found the gems. Rhodes designated the English as ''the first race in the world'' and judging from today's twin marvels, India and South Africa.... (This isn't the place to go into the racial and radical aspects of Rhodes' life and rule, as well as the Boar Wars, that are nonetheless partially covered in my book *Homosexual Warriors*.)

Rhodes (Cecil John, 1853-1902) returned to England and entered Oxford and the

Apollo University Lodge, as did Wilde. One of his first lovers was his associate Robert Dundas Graham followed by Henry Latham Currey who treacherously married, said Rhodes who had an obsession with loyalty and trust. The boys he had, before and after Graham, were numerous, all described as splendid, none given responsibilities other than minor posts such as bodyguards. (In a film on Rhodes' life he is described as having a sexual passion for beautiful young men.) The love of his life was perhaps Neville Pickering to whom he left his fortune in his will, until a riding accident deprived him of the boy's presence, love and warmth, the lad who died in Rhodes' arms, an intolerably wrenching loss. Pickering had been attended to by Doctor Leander Starr Jameson who took Pickering's place in Rhodes' affections. It was Jameson who was to hold Rhodes to him as Rhodes passed away, age 48. Jameson himself died on a trip to England and his remains were laid to rest beside Rhodes' own, in Rhodes' grave on Malindidzimu Hill, in what I prefer to call Rhodesia.

Rhodes memorial at Devil's Peak Cape Town and his tomb.

Horatio Kitchener

Irish-born Kitchener (Horatio, 1850 – 1916) was an imminent Mason whose ship, HMS *Hampshire*, hit a German mine on its way to Russia, killing 600 on board, including Kitchener himself.

He made his bones during the battle for Khartoum, the capital of Sudan. The Sudan was in revolt, led by El Mahdi, the head of the Dervishes, fierce tribesmen who disdained death. The Dervishes were an ascetic sect that learned humility through begging, but never for themselves, as everything they collected went to others poorer than they. (The Swirling Dervishes are a small sect situated basically in Turkey and are known today as a tourist attraction.) The use of the word ''Dervish'' during Kitchener's time was a pejorative term used to describe an Islamic person who opposed the British, whether he was really a Dervish or not. Khartoum at the time was under General Charles Gordon, called by some a crackpot, by others merely mad. He loved little boys and had founded an orphanage in which he personally bathed the lads and then dried them in front of mirrors so they could admire their clean manly bodies. A Dervish army attacked Khartoum and Gordon and his men were slaughtered. This the British did not forgive and so a force under Kitchener was formed. Kitchener personally interviewed those who would serve under him, all young and handsome, called his Band of Boys, where marriage was a bar to entry. One of his purported lovers was his secretary Oswald Fitzgerald, and he was fond of the handsome Frank ''Brat'' Maxwell. About Kitchener the reporter George Ernest Morrison relayed the words of a Reuter correspondent: Kitchener ''has the failing acquired by most Egyptian officers, a taste for buggery.'' Another of Kitchener's handsome favorites was the son of a Canadian judge, the engineer Edouard Girouard. He was responsible for building a railroad across the desert, a job he did brilliantly. When Kitchener was told that the engines rounded up were so old that they could blow up and kill those next to them, Kitchener responded that they could assume a few incidental casualties.

Kitchener with Fitz, Edouard Girouard, and ''Brat'' Maxell.

Kitchener was given permission to avenge Gordon. He attacked the Dervishes in several localities, and although incredibly outnumbered, the discipline of his troops, their cannon and Maxims (the first machine guns), mowed down file and file after file of the heedless attackers. Kitchener treated the press as drunken scum, ordering them out of his way, while an aid, Hector Macdonald, gave them breakfast and even allowed them to bath in his facilities, personally handing them a towel. Macdonald came out smelling like a rose, while Kitchener was called a barbarian for the way he let his men slaughter the wounded Dervish survivors, and parade their leader in chains. The Khartoum tomb of Mahdi, a man who had become sacred to the Dervish, was destroyed and his bones thrown into the Nile. Kitchener wanted to keep the skull and have it mounted in silver as a drinking cup, but news got out and he was forced to have it buried.

Kitchener became such a hero that he was awarded peerage and given £30,000, an immense sum. His face appeared on postcards, biscuit tins and buttons, and he was idolized by every schoolboy. As for Macdonald, he was later discharged of his duties for homosexuality, sent to London where he was court marshaled. The scandal was such that he fled to Paris where, seeing his name on the front pages of kiosk newspapers, he returned to his room and fired a bullet into his brain. Macdonald's full story can be found in my book *Homosexual Heroes*.

Kitchener replaced commander Lord Roberts at the end of the Boer Wars in 1900. The Boer Wars were a result of a disgusting abuse of British power. The Boers were already in the region of the Cape when the British moved in. The British wanted to protect their route to the Indies, and to benefit from the mines--diamonds and gold--whose discovery took place, bit by bit, over a score of years. They were also in competition with other powers who were seeking a foothold in Africa, notably the French, Germans, Belgians and Portuguese. The nature of the Boer, intensely independent farmers, made cohabitation impossible, although that was what the English at first strove for, along the lines of a federation that existed in Canada between the English and the French.

The Boers moved inland, their territory, the Transvaal Republic, accepted by the British in the Convention of 1852, and the Orange Free State, recognized by the Convention of 1854. When gold and diamonds were discovered in these areas the British simply annexed both entities, the beginning of the abuse that would see 26,000 Boers killed in British concentration camps, 81% of them children, the rest women (the men having been killed or exiled).

There was little the Boers could do as they found themselves between two forces, the Zulu to the north and the British to the south. To fight both would have been suicidal. But later the British took events in hand by defeating the Zulu, leaving the Boers free to confront the British.

The catalyst came in 1880 over a tax a single Boer refused to pay. He attacked the tax collector and later, when troops arrived, his friends attacked them. The Boers had no standing army but when necessity demanded it, they formed militias they called Commandos and chose leaders. There was no all-out war, properly speaking, but short skirmishes which introduced the British to Boer snipers, to Boer ambushes, Boer mobility and, for the first time, guerrilla warfare.

The Boers were farmers, as said, who lived in the saddle and ate thanks to their marksmanship, making them the best fighters in the world. A good time for a Boer was a reunion of friends during which there was a competition aimed at shooting eggs from the top of fence posts at a distance of 100 yards. In contrast, the Brits wore red jackets and sometimes kilts, but they were also armed with iron discipline.

The first battles were won by the Boers. At Laing's Nek 150 out of 480 Brits died. At Schuinshoogte 139 Brits were lost, half the number that had been sent out. The worst was Majuba during which hundreds died, while the Boers lost 1 killed and 4 wounded. Yet the British had a homeland from which the cannon fodder was quasi limitless. The Boers, of Dutch descent, had nothing since their home country had been rendered impotent following the Napoleonic Wars, a handicap that would eventually turn the tide.

This, the First Boer War, came to an end in 1881. Britain withdrew from the annexed territories.

In 1886 the world's greatest deposit of gold was discovered 30 miles from Pretoria, the Boer capital. It was this discovery that pushed the British to engage all its forces when the Second Boer War broke out in 1899. The problem was that a new town had sprung up near the mines, Johannesburg, expanded with non-Boers, there for the gold. The Boers were now a distinct minority. So the ultra-British Cape Prime Minister Cecil Rhodes decided to take Johannesburg, knowing that the "outsiders", as the non-Boer inhabitants were called, would rise up against the Boers who, trying to keep power despite their lessening numbers, had deprived the outsiders of their right to vote, among other things. 600 men tried to take Johannesburg. 65 were killed by the Boers who lost 1 man. In defeat, Rhodes was forced to resign as Prime Minister of the Cape. The man who had been in charge of the raid was Leander Jameson. He and other captives were sent to London by the Boers to be tried. Although London was responsible for the raid, it denied the fact following the defeat of Rhodes, and the prisoners were given jail terms. At the end of his, Jameson returned to a hero's welcome and was made Prime Minister of the Cape.

During the peace that followed the raid on Johannesburg the Boer Kruger decided to prepare for all eventualities. He bought 37,000 of the most modern rifles, 50 million rounds of ammunition and the latest Krupp cannon. He then equipped an army of 25,000 men. After Rhodes' raid London had decided that war with the Boers should be avoided. They nonetheless demanded that the Boers treat the ''outsiders'', many of which were English, more equitably. London also wanted the blacks to be better treated, which was far from the case. Kruger was so certain that war was immanent he declared it himself, on the 11 of October 1899. In London this brought peals of laughter.

The Boers, deeply religious, had no wish to fight, especially against fellow English Protestants. Yet they encircled Ladysmith, Kimberley and Mafeking, defended by Baden-Powell. Military historians later noted that this was a terrible mistake on the part of the Boers, and that every Boer siege during the First Boer War had ended in disaster for the Boers. It seemed that the Boers, individualists, simply lacked all notion of strategy.

British reinforcements arrived, and headed for the towns under siege. But even then the Boers continued to decimate them, killing hundreds and wounding thousands, while they never lost more than a dozen dead. Back in London there were no more peals of laughter when families were made aware of the loss of their loved ones, lovers, brothers, husbands and fathers. The British commanding general, Buller, was called Sir

Reverse for obtaining the opposite of what he had set out to do.

In 1900 Britain sent the largest force ever to cross the seas, 180,000 men, Field Marshal Roberts in charge. Thanks to these immense forces the Boers began to retreat. When a force reached Mafeking and freed Baden-Powell, all Britain broke out in celebration. When Roberts captured Pretoria in September 1900 he declared the war over and Boer lands were officially annexed.

While hated in Britain, the Boers were applauded in Europe, and Queen Wilhelmina of the Netherlands sent a ship to pick up Kruger. He later went to Switzerland where he died in 1904. Those not so lucky, a total of 26,000 Boer prisoners of war, were exiled to St. Helena (5,000), Ceylon and India.

What followed was the harshest of tragedies. The Boers decided on guerrilla warfare, and by December 1900, just three months after the war was supposed to have ended, 1,500 Brits had become casualties to the Boer offensive. To fight them, the British invented the blockhouse, each manned by 5 to 8 soldiers, and so effective that no bridge near a blockhouse was ever blown up.

British blockhouse

Kitchener, now in charge, ordered a scorched earth punishment. All Boer farms were burned to the ground. The wells were poisoned. The fields salted. Women and children were rounded up. 26,000 would die in the camps set up for them. Malnutrition, endemic diseases--measles, typhoid, cholera-- and dysentery put Kitchener in the category of the swine that slaughtered the 8,000 boys at Srebrenica. What Kitchener and Baden-Powell purportedly did, sexually, to the children then and in India is, if true, but a footnote in these two despicable lives. Naturally, when a British soldier lost a friend to Boer guerrilla tactics he would want to take it out on as many Boer recruits as possible, but their aim was never the death of women and children through concentration-camp neglect. Arthur Conan Doyle was in Africa too, a volunteer doctor at a field hospital in

Bloemfontein. He sided with Kitchener's stringent conditions, pointing out that 14,000 British soldiers died too from disease while 8,000 died fighting. He didn't point out that had the British respected the Conventions of 1852 and 1854, had they not groveled before the scintillation of gold and diamonds, not one England lad would have forfeited his precious life.

Decimated, exiled, their farms burned and the fields salted, the Boers wound up working in the mines. From there after the economy of South Africa was and is based on gold and diamonds.

This, then, is the history behind the Boer Wars. Like the Jews fleeing pharaoh, the Boers had trekked north to establish the Orange Free State, as said, while others found their Palestine in Natal, beyond the Drakensbert Mountains. They had emigrated with their slaves, refusing British abolition of slavery. The Boer's major assets had been mobility, confidence in the individual and superb marksmanship, but the discovery of gold and diamonds in these areas sealed their fate.

In 1902 Kitchener was named

commander-in-chief in India. When the First World War broke out he was appointed Secretary of State for War. Kitchener had difficulty getting along with other members of the government, who called him obstinate, impossible, a slippery fish and a liar--or, more diplomatically, ''his veracity left much to be desired''. During an inspection tour he took the seals of his office with him so that he couldn't be sacked during his absence. In 1916, as stated in the first paragraph, he was blown to smithereens when his ship hit a mine launched by a German U-boat. Conspiracy theories popped up, some blaming Churchill (for which Douglas was sent to jail for defamation, as explained elsewhere), others the Jews, still others Irish Republicans. As for Kitchener, his body was never recovered.

Kitchener's homosexuality was already a matter of discussion during his time in Khartoum when someone said, as related, that his acquaintance with Arabs enhanced his ''taste for buggery.'' For the last three years of his life Kitchener had ''been living openly'' with his aide-de-camp, Captain Oswald Fitzgerald, with whom he vanished on the *Hampshire*. His biographer John Pollock states that as a young man ''he was not like other boys," and as a young military officer he was "never one of the guys," preferring to bond with a single "inseparable companion"--usually slightly older--until his fifties when the boys he chose as aides were young and handsome. In 1908 Kitchener was named a homosexual in Edward Stevenson's book *The Intersexes*. There are some men who completely deny even the existence of women. Kitchener and Walt Whitman were such men, although Queen Victoria remarked, "They claimed he disliked women, but I can only say he was very nice to me." He and Fitz remodeled his country house, Broome Court, and Kitchener said that had he not become a general he would have chosen interior decorating as his life's work.

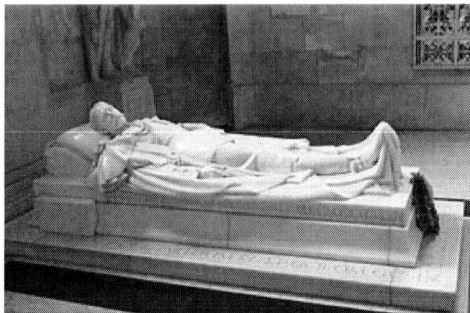

Kitchener memorial St. Paul Cathedral, London.

Richard Burton
John Speke

Richard Francis Burton (1821 – 1890) was an eminent Freemason explorer. The catalyst for the expeditions of Richard Burton and John Speke was the Greek geographer known as Ptolemy who in 150 A.D. produced a map which showed, thanks to information gleaned by the Greek explorer Diogenes, the existence of a mountain range with twin peaks, from which two rivers flowed to form the Nile. Burton took on Speke in his attempt to find the mountains and the exact sources of the Nile. The Nile had posed problem since the pharaohs. It not only crosses the most desolate, hottest deserts in the world, it not only never dried up in summer, but, against all logic, it flooded Egypt during the hottest months, making Egypt the breadbasket of the ancient world, the reason for its being a prime Roman conquest, as well as giving Cleopatra sway over Caesar and Marc Antony.

Ptolemy's map

Burton, tall and swarthy, had become known when he successfully made a hajj to Mecca, disguised as an Arab merchant. Aged 37, he went so far as to have himself circumcised, an extraordinarily painful process during adulthood. Mecca was, and is today, a city closed to infidels. Had he been caught, he would have been torn to pieces. He certainly had one of the richest sex lives known to western man: Already, as an adolescent, he and his older brother accompanied their father, a hypochondriac, throughout Europe in search of spas. While he took the waters the two boys entertained themselves in a steady succession of whorehouses. It was Burton who translated and brought to us the *Kama Sutra*, the content of which he had turned into practical knowledge since his balls dropped. That he would go on to boy-love was interpreted as a step towards Nirvana.

The first question that comes to mind concerning the discovery of the origin of the Nile is simply why not sail up the river to its source? This had been tried in 1850 by Andrew Melly, a millionaire who died of fever. In 1851 Andrea De Bono made his way up the cataracts, selling captured lions and human beings, until stopped by malaria. Giovanni Miani tried in 1860, paying his passage by selling ivory but turned back too due to malaria and hostile tribes. Now it was Burton's turn.

Burton could apparently speak Arabic and Persian so well he could pass for someone from both peoples. He is said to have spoken 29 other languages, including Hindustani, Gujarati, Punjabi, Sinhi, Saraiki, Marathi, Sanskrit, Portuguese, Spanish, German, Icelandic, Swahili, Hebrew, Aramaic, Latin, Greek, French and Italian. He believed in British superiority (as did Rhodes), a normal sentiment in that the British were everywhere on the planet and everywhere successful. He loved the desert and Arab dress.

Speke was as tall as Burton, 6 feet, had blue eyes and light hair. Even later, when they were implacable enemies, Burton described him as being courageous, perseverant and energetic. Burton wore a black beard and a perpetual brooding expression. Their first experience together was harrowing:

Somalia then, as today, had a notorious reputation for violence, founded, it seems, on their seizing a man's genitals and unmanning him with a single thrust of a knife. Burton, Speke and two aids had camped along the shore of the Somalian town of Berbera. Perhaps because it was feared that they were a British vanguard whose purpose was to deprive the Somalians of their wealth--their slave trade--or perhaps simply to steal their possessions, the explorers' two tents were attacked in the early morning. There were four men in two tents, Burton, William Stroyan, Speke and G.E. Herne. Hearing someone outside his and Burton's tent, Stroyan went out and was immediately hit on the head with a sword while a spear was thrust through his heart. Burton exited and received a spear that pierced him from one cheek through the other, destroying teeth and cutting across the roof of his mouth. Speke had come out of his tent firing, his gun killing several Arabs until he was wrestled to the ground and tied. He later wrote that when someone groped at his privates he was certain that they would be cut off. Instead, to Speke's inexpressible relief, the man was only searching the area preferred by Arabs when hiding knives. Nevertheless a man ran up and planted his spear into Speke's chest, several times, the last thrust aimed at Speke's heart that he was able to deflect with his tied hands, badly injuring them. The man, furious, jabbed the spear into his thigh, to the bone. Knowing this was the end, Speke righted himself and ran down the beach through a hail of spears. He found Burton and Herne pushing off in a boat. He joined them and they rowed across to Aden, under British rule. Miraculously, Speke was back on his feet in a few weeks. Burton's wounds would take months to heal.

Facially scarred for life, Burton and Speke set out for Zanzibar. Both men were alike in one instance, they both had dominating mothers, and fathers in retreat. Fathers, absent due to work, alcoholism or who die early, coupled with the aforementioned mothers, are classic in the creation of homosexuals, although this is far from being a full-proof formula. Otherwise both men were totally different. Only in one instance did Speke lose his head and strike a porter; Burton regularly beat his. Burton hated Africans, Speke, like Livingston, genuinely liked them. It would turn out that Speke was often right in his premonitions. He wanted, for example, to explore Lake Victoria, the veritable source of the Nile, before Lake Tanganyika, while Burton agreed with their sponsor, the Royal Geographical Society, that an inland ''sea'' the Society had just become aware of, Lake Tanganyika, should come first. Speke did make the mistake, however, of cutting back on sums spent on beads and cloth, absolutely essential in buying food and paying passage through hostile lands, which caused huge problems later. He refused, too, to buy a portable boat, a miscalculation that would land them in trouble multiple times.

In Zanzibar they recruited around 140 men. When they shoved off for the mainland the British consul, a thoroughly good man, whispered to Speke, ''Good luck. I would not travel with that man (Burton) under any condition.'' How Speke felt about Burton at the time is unknown because Burton was his superior, and it was Burton who had chosen him over hundreds of other candidates. That said, Speke had nevertheless made it known to intimates that Burton had sexually propositioned him, a possibility that, knowing what we known about Speke's honesty, we have no reason to doubt.

Burton

The Royal Geographical Society wanted both men to bring back specimens of animals and plants. Burton didn't hesitate to broaden the mandate to include anthropological discoveries, including the measurement of native penises (although he hated the natives to see him naked because what they saw inevitably brought on mirth). For his part, Speke examined vaginas, and commented on those sewn shut until the girls' suitors saw fit to force them.

They made their way over and through incredible physical obstacles, forests, deserts, torrents and marshes. The same was true of diseases, especially smallpox that slaughtered thousands, malaria and ulcers (chiefly of the feet and ankles), although they would both come back alive, which was far from the case of those who lost their lives in Africa, about whom we know little because they hadn't succeeded. In Burton's case he came down with a sickness that deprived him of the use of his arms and legs, for four months, leaving him unable to walk without aid for a further eleven. Speke nearly went blind, and for months had to be led by hand. Strangely, his eyes got better when, trying to extract an insect from his ear, he did himself such harm that his face, down to his shoulder, ''became contorted,'' in Speke's words. But the infected area seemed to have drawn away the infection from his eyes.

They made it to Tanganyika, the first whites ever. (When an Arab was told of the ''discovery'' of the lake he said, ''What are you talking about? We've known it was there for generations!'') They stayed in a town on the lake, Ujiji, where Stanley would soon meet Livingston, a center of Arab slave and ivory trade. They were offered girls by their parents, the price being nothing more than a loincloth.

John Speke

They had heard from several travelers that at the northern end of Tanganyika there was a river that flowed out of it, supposedly the source of the Nile. Boats were hired and Burton, extremely sick, went there with Speke. Alas, either the reports had been false or Burton and Speke had made a mistake in understanding--Burton claimed that Speke spoke no African languages, and as for

Burton, his Arabic had been tested by an Arabist who found it rudimentary, but he was tested again by a friend who found it excellent. Burton's fluency in African language is not known. There was indeed a river, but it flowed *into* Lake Tanganyika. Disappointed, they returned to Ujiji where it was decided that Speke alone, with porters, would investigate the huge lake to the northeast, Lake Victoria. Hiring a boat, he navigated to the north of the lake where he found a river that flowed *out* of it, to the north, the beginning of the Nile. When Speke returned to tell Burton, Burton fell into days of depression. They returned to Zanzibar, both so sick they were carried into the town. From there Speke made his way to what should have been glory. Burton, ill, followed later.

No one will ever take from Speke the fact that it was he--due to Burton's illness--who first made the vitally important discovery of the source of the Nile. Yet today there is one biography of Speke, half a dozen of Burton. The reason seems to be due to a simple promise: Speke had given his word not to go to the Royal Geographical Society without Burton. But he did so. Burton accused him of being a lying cad, following up his accusation by belittling him to RGS members, by giving interviews poisoning Speke's well, and later by writing books in which he smeared Speke. Speke, less audible, was soon vilified. Added to this was Speke's early death, just six years after his discovery. Once underground, Burton let out all stops in his vilification. Had Burton not been crippled they would have found the source of the Nile together. As it is today, the name of Burton is known by all, that of Speke known to a few.

Burton and Speke were among those in a line, a very long line, of courageous, thoroughly fearless, totally indomitable, curious, tenacious and wonderfully intelligent British who made Britain the world's greatest power for generations. Speke and his later aid James Grant were, in addition, thoroughly good men.

While Burton was struck down by illness, Speke trekked to Lake Victoria and discovered the source of the Nile, an enigma as old as the pharaohs, as related. Burton at first admitted as much before lambasting Speke, putting in doubt his discovery and labeling him a disloyal liar. Speke had divulged that Burton had hit on him and Burton, for his part, insinuated that Speke himself was an in-the-closet homosexual.

While stationed in India General Napier had asked Burton to visit three local whorehouses supposedly frequented by British soldiers, whose prostitutes were exclusively boys. Whether Napier had made the request to Burton because he was aware of Burton's sexual proclivities, or whether it was due to his excellence in languages, is unknown. There was a Napier Report, but whether it was on paper or delivered orally is also unknown, as the report is lost to us. The precision of the report is such that Burton is believed to have been a participant in the sexual happenings. The contrary would be surprising as Burton was by then known by one and all for his no-holds-barred sexuality. In an often-cited passage of the report, Burton reveals that uncastrated boys were preferred (many of the prostitutes were eunuchs) because one could grab their balls and use them as reins in guiding the movement of the lads' buttocks. Although such recondite knowledge is beyond my personal understanding, it does indicate that Burton followed what was going on from close up.

Burton later went on to give us a version

of the *Kama Sutra* and the *Arabian Nights* in 16 volumes (!), and he was working on what he called his *magnum opus, The Scented Garden*, already 1,282 pages long, *said to have been* a defense of homosexual activity. Some suggest that he never touched his wife *in that way*, but she was devoted to him to the end. She had him given last rights, maintaining that he was still alive, despite his heart attack at age 69. The possibility of his still being alive is refuted by most. At any rate, Burton was an atheist, and her ignoring his wishes to be buried with no religious rites is in itself an act of ignorant barbarity, one enforced by her destroying his *magnum opus* and his other ''filth'' as she called it.

After his discovery of Lake Victoria Speke returned there to glean additional proof of its being the source of the Nile, in the company of James Grant. Part of the journey was through the land of a king whose family had reigned supreme over the enormous region for 400 years. His capital was known for its huge structures, its clean streets and a superb agricultural system that had banished famine since living memory. He had never seen a white man and when he heard that Speke was coming with presents, he sacrificed

400 of his subjects in thanks. When presented with guns he had Speke try one out on four cows that Speke, a renowned marksman and avid hunter, immediately shot dead. The king then gave a rifle to a child and told him to kill the first man he came across outside the king's huge complex of huts. The child came back, laughing, mission accomplished. Speke assisted, helpless, as one to three of the king's wives were led away, daily, to have their heads bashed in, for errors in kingly etiquette, such as the wife who served a certain kind of fruit that another, specific wife, was supposed to give him. The king used Speke for sexual advice, unsatisfied with both the length and endurance of his member. For endurance, Speke told him the less often he honored his wives the stronger would be his lust. As for size, the king had Speke draw him nude which, if the drawing is exact, left the king with decidedly non-African dimensions. Anyway, Speke told the king that a stick of any length did the job, but the king didn't believe a word.

James Grant

The king's mother, enormously fat, also desired Speke's medical knowledge and didn't hesitate to strip naked for his examination. He gave her quinine and counsel, thanks for which she offered him two girls. There seems no doubt that Speke had them both, and he fell in love with one, but was repulsed when she admitted that her interest went only as far as his wealth.

Speke eventually got back to Lake Victoria and returned with proof that he had been right. But it was Burton who received a knighthood. As a final humiliation Burton organized a debate between them both, moderated by Livingston, Livingston who also believed that Speke was mistaken about the source of the Nile, this because Speke and

Grant hadn't descended the river far enough from Lake Victoria to convince him (the reason Livingston would soon leave the find the veritable source himself, leading to his disappearance and ''discovery'' by Stanley, and Livingston's ultimate death).

The day before the debate, Speke went hunting, his favorite pastime. He laid his shotgun against a wall that he climbed up on. He then reached down to retrieve it by the barrow. Somehow it went off, shooting him through the upper chest. The day before he had been with Burton and Livingston to plan the debate, but certain that both men would do what they could to demean him, he had stormed out shouting ''I've had enough!'' Now, dead, the rumor was that he had taken his own life, although most people doubt that Speke, who had suffered so greatly during his expeditions, would have done such a thing. Others felt that he was at the end of his rope and did, indeed, kill himself.

Burton's wife had a tent monument raised above both their graves. Speke was honored with an obelisk.

Spike's Obelisk/Burton's Tomb

THE ORDER OF CHAERONEA
338 B.C. and 1897
George Cecil Ives – Sacred Band –
Montague Summers, John
Gambril Nicholson, Alec Milling

Erected by Thebans in memory of the
300 lovers and belovèds that fell before Philip
and his son Alexander the Great in 338 B.C.,
the Lion of Chaeronea was restored by British

archeologist Cecil Harcourt Smith, thanks to funds from the Order of Chaeronea in 1902. Nearby are the cremated remains of Philip's Macedonian soldiers.

The Order of Chaeronea was founded in 1897 by George Cecil Ives who himself best described its aim: ''We believe in the glory of passion. We believe in the inspiration of emotion. We believe in the holiness of love.''

The Order of Chaeronea founder.

They also believed in erotic passion between men, and although they went out of their way to deny that their Order was a means to meet like-minded and like-bodied mates, that's exactly what took place, as they subconsciously knew it would. Oscar Wilde and his paramour Douglas were members.

The Order was named after the Battle of
Chaeronea, during which the Sacred Band of
Thebes was defeated by Alexander the Great
and his father Philip, in the year 338 B.C.,
from which date the order delineated time, as
we do A.D., meaning that this year, 2019 is, by
the Order's calculation, 2357.

As the story of the Sacred Band is of
infinitely more interest than the secret society
that honored it, I'm now going to make a
detour into that blessed epoch, where men and
boys were free to live their love--were
encouraged to do so--under the azure skies of
Hellas and the tepid breath of the North
Wind, he who had robbed Apollo of the love
of Hyacinth by killing the boy with a discus
the North Wind deviated from its course, all
because the Spartan lad wouldn't give the
Wind a tumble.

The Sacred Band destroyed the Spartan
army in 371 B.C., the first army to ever do so.
The Spartans had been victorious against the
Persians and had brought Athens to its knees
during the Peloponnesian Wars. And now a
group of Thebans destroyed its power forever.
The cause of the war between the Spartans
and Thebans was Spartan domination over a

people that wanted its freedom, a people who had had enough of Spartans ever trying to force them into forming an oligarchy, always threatening their very existence. The Thebans elected a general, Epaminondas, to confront them at the town of Leuctra. The outcome swung back and forth until Epaminondas gave the signal for his lover, Pelopidas, to enter the fray at the head of the Sacred Band of Thebes, lovers and their belovèds, who would unhesitatingly fight to the death rather than show themselves cowards in front of their comrades, and, especially, before he who had been chosen as a life companion, first as a lover, then as a friend. The Thebans allowed the Spartan survivors to leave with their dead, including their king, Cleombrotus, and then raised a trophy to their victory. When the Spartans learned of the defeat the families of the dead rejoiced, those whose sons had survived wept in humiliation. But here the real victory was not over the Spartans, the veritable victory was the loyalty and friendship--the pledge of eternal love--begun years prior when Epaminondas had met the young, handsome and valiant Pelopidas, a truly unique figure in Greek history. Born rich and dedicated to attaining the summits in athletics, Pelopidas squandered the family fortune on Theban poor. Plutarch tells us that when criticized for dilapidating his wealth, reminding him that money was a basic necessity, Pelopidas pointed to a blind and crippled pauper and said, ''Yes, it's necessary for him.'' He himself ate the simplest of foods and wore the plainest clothes. He rejoiced in the hardships of physical and militaristic training which took place in an atmosphere of soldierly friendships.

Epaminondas not only won at Leuctra, he and Pelopidas then entered the Peloponnese where they set free the Messenian helots, after generations of slavery. Naturally, Messenia became Thebes' most loyal and most grateful supporter. In all, Epaminondas was destined to enter the Peloponnese *four* times to put down Sparta's attempts to re-enslave the helots. After the Battle of Leuctra there were only 1,000 Spartans left. The disappearance of the Spartans was now programmed, a mere matter of time.

The Sacred Band was led by Pelopidas. He modeled it after his own personal friendship with Epaminondas, 150 lovers and 150 belovèds, men and boys who would never shy away from death if it meant betraying his lover's or his belovèd's faith. Polyaenus describes the Sacred Band as being composed of men "devoted to each other by mutual obligations of love", and Plato describes a lover as being ''a friend inspired by god.'' The Theban general Pammenes had criticized Nestor of Trojan War fame when he organized his troops by tribe and clan and not by lovers and belovèds because, says Plutarch, ''Friendship grounded in love is never to be broken and is invincible, since lovers and belovèds, to avoid shame, will rush into danger to rescue one another.'' Pammenes himself organized his army in such a way that lovers were always together. The perfect example was given during the Battle of Leuctra when one of the Sacred Band, ambushed, asked the enemy to run him through at the breast so his lover would not blush at seeing a wound to the back. The Sacred Band never sought death for itself. To the contrary, they entered battle protected with armor and armed with the finest weapons. They spent their days in the palaestra training and learning strategy, but also in philosophy and singing and dancing. There was much discussion on tactics, a science Epaminondas was already famous for. Their bodies were sleek, oiled and kept clean by their companion who scraped the oil from the toned muscles with a strigil. They sweated in huts warmed by fired stones over which they splashed water. Plato tells us that ''love between males was so special in Thebes that it was illegal for anyone to maintain that sex between men was *not* beautiful.'' The Sacred Band was stationed on the Acropolis. Their service started at around age twenty and ended around age thirty. Pelopidas turned them into shock troops whose main function was killing enemy leaders by any means possible, thereby crippling the enemy by depriving it of its head.

Cicero called Epaminondas ''the first man of Greece.'' Centuries later Montaigne named Epaminondas as being one of three of the world's ''worthiest men,'' the other two being Homer and Alexander the Great. Most aspects of Epaminondas's reputation have been lost in the mists of time due to the fact that just a score of years after his passing Alexander obliterated Thebes, thusly destroying his and Pelopidas's heritage. He is also less known because we have, thanks to Plutarch (see Sources), the life of Pelopidas, while that of Epaminondas was lost. But we do have traces of his past due to Cornelius Nepos (see Sources) and Diodorus Siculus. As a boy he favored wrestling, running and prowess in the handling of weapons. What the poets call the defining moment of his life occurred during the Battle of Mantinea, in 385 B.C., an earlier battle when Thebes fought on the side of Sparta. Here he saved Pelopidas's life. Epaminondas had noticed the boy in camp, and when he came upon him during the fighting, slumped on the ground amid the bodies of his comrades, apparently dead as his body had been pierced in six places by sword and spear thrusts. Epaminondas stood his ground above him, he too receiving wounds to the chest by a spear and on the arm by a sword. He in turn was saved by the Spartan king Agesipolis who arrived in the nick of time with his men. Times change as do alliances and Thebes found itself fighting innumerable skirmishes against the Spartans until the city-state was forced to bend to Spartan will.

Of the two, Epaminondas was devoted to study and philosophizing, Pelopidas to the hunt and physical training in the palaestra, encouraging physical relations between boys as a way of inspiring one's companions to greater heights of effort.

Epaminondas and Pelopidas would make a specialty of disguised assassination, as they had in retaking Thebes. Their conspirators, a total of 48 in number, had arranged a drinking party for Spartans and Sparta's allies, the chief nobles of Thebes, an orgy in which Pelopidas had sent friends wearing women's garb over their weapons, the faces disguised under garlands, Plutarch inform us, who fell upon the enemy, many of whom were naked and defenseless. They then went to the homes of other nobles and surprised them in their beds. Some of these fought bravely, and in one house the man who preceded Pelopidas was mortally wounded by someone who had seized his dagger, whom Pelopidas then ran through with his sword. Plutarch mentioned that the weather had helped the assailants, as the wind and snow lured the enemy into a false sense of security, and encouraged them in pastimes of drinking and sexual sporting in the confines of their rooms.

Although the Spartan force was 1,500, it was in disarray because no one knew what was going on. This gave Epaminondas and Pelopidas time to round up priests who went through the city, mobilizing the people whose one wish was to rid themselves of the Spartans.

Pelopidas and the Sacred Band had many valorous moments, but the height of their glory took place in 376 when the 300 came across a Spartan army of 1,800. The battle was so one-sided that one of Pelopidas's men cried out, ''We have fallen into Spartan hands.'' ''No,'' countered Pelopidas, ''they have fallen into ours.'' Both phalanxes met with destructive force, but it was the Sacred Band that pierced that of the Spartans, then turning to decimate their exposed flanks. The Spartans fled, the very first time they had been defeated by a small force.

In a dream Pelopidas had been told to sacrifice a chestnut-haired virgin in order to win the above battle against the Spartans, as Agamemnon had sacrificed his daughter Iphigenia (3) and as Themistocles had been said to have made a human sacrifice before the Battle of Salamis (3). As Pelopidas hesitated, a chestnut mare suddenly entered his camp causing the Theban augur Theocritus to shout out, ''Dear friend, this is the gods' gift, this is the sacrificial virgin!''

After this brief résumé introducing Epaminondas and Pelopidas, we can go into detail.

Epaminondas and Pelopidas.

If Sparta had become more powerful after the Peloponnesian Wars (3), so had Thebes, who flexed its muscles more and more in its sphere of influence: Boeotia. Thebes decided to align itself with other states to counter Sparta's new self-confidence. It therefore joined in a war against Spartans in 395, along with Athens, Corinth and Argos, called the Corinthian War, that they all lost to such an extent that they were forced to again ally themselves to Sparta.

Then in 382, while in the vicinity of Thebes, the Spartan commander Phoebidas decided to take advantage of unrest within the city to occupy the Cadmea, the Acropolis. The Spartans set up a puppet regime but, incredibly, allowed Epaminondas to remain within the walls because he was poor and the Spartans equated his poverty with impotence. Other Thebans had been forced to leave, among them Pelopidas. Both men, one inside and one outside, now prepared those around them for a revolt against the Spartans. When ready, Pelopidas led his men into the city where, with the aid of his lover, they killed the city's governing body in their beds. They then set siege to the Cadmea. The Spartans, in a rare move for them, agreed to surrender if they could leave with their lives. This was granted and Thebes was again free.

Epaminondas and Pelopidas then went to the shrine of Iolaus where they offered up thanks. Iolaus had been a member of the Argonauts and one of Heracles' lovers (12). Heracles offered the boy, then age sixteen, to his wife, age thirty, with whom he had a child. The gymnasium in Thebes was called the Iolaus and athletic games to the boy were known as the Iolaeia. Plutarch states that men and their belovèds exchanged sacred vows of love at the shrine of Iolaus. And according to Aristotle, same-sex couples ''invoked his name to guarantee their oaths of faith and to punish faithless lovers.''

It's amusing to note that during the games--Nemean, Panathenaea or Olympic--''boys never touched women or other boys in the whole period when they are at the peak of their training,'' wrote Plutarch. Just like today. (An amusing anecdote comes to us concerning the Theban athlete Cleitomachus, a champion boxer, who pushed sexual abstinence so far as to turn his eyes away from dogs coupling.)

Between 378 and 371 Sparta sent out two armies to subdue Thebes, the first, headed by King Cleombrotus, immediately returned, due to inauspicious omens, the second by King Agesilaus II came up against a trench and wall Thebans had constructed around the city. The Spartan siege was soon abandoned so the Spartans could return home to keep an eye on their slaves, the helots.

Thebes was now free to rid every Boeotian city of its oligarchies, replaced by Theban democracy. An attempt at peace was made between Thebes and Sparta in 371 but

Thebes wanted to sign for all of Boeotia, which the Spartans refused, saying that each state had to decide its destiny for itself. In that case, Thebes replied, Sparta could not sign for all of Laconia, home of the Spartans.

The Battle of Leuctra, although of vital importance, will not be given in detail because we know so little. The Spartans may have had 11,000 men and the Theban's 6,000. Whereas the Thebans were certain they would lose, they were nonetheless made up of the Sacred Band, all 300 decided to die to the last, as well as the other 5,700 similarly bent on mass suicide if that were needed to show the Sacred Band that they too were men. The Spartans were made up of troops from different regions, few of which were Spartans. We know that the tactics of Epaminondas were professional for he was the finest captain in Greece, and we know that he was perfectly seconded by the cavalry of Pelopidas.

The Spartan king Cleombrotus, Pausanias's son, fell nearly immediately, proof of the valiance of Spartan leaders who headed their men. Perhaps this caused a rout because at the end of the day 400 Spartans and 1,000 of their troops lay sprawled over the fields. The Spartans demanded a truce to bury their dead, the immutable sign that it was they the vanquished.

A runner went off to bring Athens the good news, so sure of himself that he had donned a wreath of laurels, only to find somber silence. The Spartans were bad, but the Athenians knew they would one day soon come up against the Thebans whom they feared far more.

Whatever fear Thebes inspired, that threat lay in the future and for the moment Spartan representatives were made *persona non grata* everywhere, or nearly. Even in the Peloponnese Sparta's most loyal ally, Tegea, revolted and chose democracy. Nearby Mantinea revolted and fortified its walls and even diverted a river so that it would encompass them on all sides, like a moat. New leagues sprang up everywhere in preparation should Sparta dare raise its serpent head still again.

So when Epaminondas decided to strike off that head once and for all, most fell over backwards to give him troops. He went onto Messenia and freed the hysterically joyful Messenians. With his own hands Epaminondas put down the first stone for what would be the new city of Messene, where exiles from all over the world would be able to return, as the Jews would centuries later to Jerusalem. Their enslavement had come to an end, years of unimaginable suffering, where any helot could be killed at any time by a Spartan, where the Spartan secret services chose those they most feared and had them assassinated, during the night, by a Spartan boy so he could make his bones, as a lad today kills and guts his first deer. This is known historically as the first invasion of Sparta.

During the second invasion in 369 Epaminondas was aided by Argives, whom he joined by forcing his way across the Isthmus defended by Sparta, Corinth, Megara and by Athenians. This short campaign resulted only in the despoiling of Spartan territory. In 367 Epaminondas marched into Thessaly where his lover Pelopidas had been taken prisoner by Alexander of Pherae. Epaminondas had sent Pelopidas as an ambassador to gain Alexander's support in future campaigns. Epaminondas didn't want to push Alexander so far that out of desperation he would kill Pelopidas, so Epaminondas simply went from town to town and massacred the populations until Alexander gave up Pelopidas.

Epaminondas and Pelopidas virtually governed Thebes together, Pelopidas, with the fire of youth, was recognized as the most aggressive of the two in his support of measures that systematically reduced Spartan strength throughout the region. Incredibly, Epaminondas was put on trial when he returned to Thebes for a crime punishable by death. To understand what went on, one has to know that Greeks held to certain principles, principles that were of vital importance to them, but at times made them lose the overall perspective of things, an example of not being able to see the forest for the trees. Epaminondas's crime was that during his expedition to Sparta to free the helots he had remained in power a little longer than the time when his term in office expired. So at his trial Epaminondas read out a prepared statement. He told the Thebans that after putting him to death they were to raise a stele in his honor on which it would be inscribed that here lies Epaminondas who saved the Thebans from Spartan tyranny at the Battle of Leuctra and then went on to chase them back to the Peloponnese, thusly saving all of Greece from their tyranny, before invading said Peloponnese in order to liberate their slaves, the helots.

Luckily for Epaminondas, the Thebans had more of a sense of humor than did the Athenians. They broke out in laughter and freed their savior. Of course, all of this is highly abridged. In truth, what happened to Epaminondas throughout all his life is what happened to every important man throughout all of Greece, from Themistocles to Pericles, as well as to even the great philosophers like Socrates: Greeks have always been jealous of other Greeks and have always tried to trip them so they would land face down in the mud. This happened time and time again to Epaminondas and Pelopidas but I won't get into the silly details. The essential is that both men always came out on top, politically speaking.

During the third invasion of the Peloponnese, in 367, Argos cleared the way for Theban troops by opening up the Isthmus. Alas, it was now that Pelopidas met his death. Epaminondas had sent him back to Pherae to put a definitive end to Alexander of Pherae. Pelopidas was at the head of a group of mercenaries who abandoned him when they took fear due to an eclipse of the sun.

Pelopidas went on anyway with a much-reduced force. He won the battle but Alexander escaped. It was during his pursuit that Pelopidas, riding ahead of his men, was waylaid and murdered. At Pelopidas's death the men cut off their hair and the manes of their horses, and took no supper. The body was buried on the battlefield in Thessaly, following pleas from the Thessalonians to be so honored.

Alexander himself, Plutarch informs us, was later assassinated by his wife, tired of his tyranny towards her: Alexander slept in a chamber at the top of a tower, the door of which was guarded by a ferocious chained dog. His wife lured the dog away and covered the steps leading to Alexander's bedroom with wool so he would not hear her three brothers approach. Alexander's body was pierced with a hundred stab wounds and thrown from the tower to the street below where it was torn to shreds by his compatriots, who also had had enough of him. Plutarch adds that the death of Alexander of Pherae ''had been too rapid''.

In 362 Epaminondas entered the Peloponnese for the fourth and last time. The target was Mantinea who had declared its independence and its support of Sparta.

Athens came to Mantinea's aid, all prepared to fight to the death against Epaminondas and Thebes, and Thebes' allies, Thessaly, Argos and Messenia. Only the word byzantine could now cover the alliances, leagues and confederations that formed and then collapsed, friends becoming deadly enemies and enemies the best of friends. A case in point was the Olympiads of 364 in which there were so many disputes that the games, the pride of all Greece, *belonging* to all Greeks, were cancelled, obliging Thebes to again send in troops who found that those who had supported them were now their bitterest foes, and democracies they had left in place were now replaced by oligarchs or by tyrants.

Before attacking Mantinea Epaminondas decided to strike at the heart of Sparta, its city. He had learned that the Spartan king Agesilaus had gone off to Mantinea, at present Sparta's closest friend, and so Epaminondas planned to enter the city ''as weak as a nest of birds,'' with Agesilaus gone. Someone had found out and sent his fastest runner to warn the Spartans who returned in time to face the arriving Thebans, all of whom were perplexed because spies had seen Agesilaus leave Sparta with their very eyes. The city was unwalled because no one had ever dared threaten the Spartans before. Only the winter-flooded Eurotas saved it, across which Spartan women, for the first time ever, saw the faces of the enemy, so unlike Athenian women and the women of literally every other Greek town who had looked on Spartans with hatred for countless years. As the bridge spanning the river was too well guarded, Epaminondas and his men went on to Mantinea. There the Athenians had just arrived. Seeing the advancing Thebans, the Athenians immediately dropped their welcoming feast and hurried out to do battle. Little by little what should have been a limited engagement turned into the biggest battle in the history of Greece, affirms Herodotus (see Sources), with a cast of thousands. Epaminondas had his troops march parallel with those of his enemy, but in a leisurely fashion, as if they didn't intend to fight that day. Some of his troops even stopped to bivouac. When he felt the enemy had sufficiently relaxed its guard, he ordered an all-out attack. Diodorus tells us that the Athenians and Spartans were undone by the rain of missiles hurled by the Sacred Band, after which, says Xenophon (see Sources), Epaminondas ''forced his army through the ranks of the enemy like the prow of a trireme.'' The Sacred Band came at the Spartans with reserve forces that broke their phalanx, forcing them to flee. The battle would have ended in a route if Epaminondas had not been fatally struck in the chest by a spear thrown from the Mantineian ranks. The spear broke, leaving the iron point deep in the heart, his death coming two years after losing Pelopidas. The Thebans immediately ended their pursuit, a testament to Epaminondas's eminence. Both sides returned their dead, and both sides put up trophies as if both had won. As was customary, Epaminondas was buried on the battlefield. He was renowned as an incorruptible man of ascetic tastes and, as he said during his trial, he had humbled Sparta and freed Messenia. The costly battle would not put an end to internecine warfare among Greeks, but this was in their nature: As Shakespeare aptly wrote, ''The fault, Brutus, is not in the stars but in ourselves.'' Epaminondas's life had been dedicated to his country and his lover, he had never married, never fathered a son to avenge his death, as Aegisthus avenged his father Thyestes, as Orestes avenged Agamemnon, as was written on the Mycenaean stele: *Son My, Avenger My.* (3)

Alas, it was then that Xenophon's son Gryllus also was struck down, in the midst of his glory, a father's intolerable loss. The Thebans returned home, no longer a danger to anyone because there was absolutely no one left to take up the torch. The body, Thebes, had been beautiful, and the Sacred Band more beautiful still, but with the head struck off, the body no longer served for anything.

As for the Spartan king Agesilaus, now very old, he did his country a final favor. He returned to Persia where he persuaded Artaxerxes to accord Sparta an enormous 230 talents in exchange for Spartan goodwill. He died returning home, his body preserved in honey. There it lies today in an undiscovered tomb--hopefully forever.

The phalanx, usually 8-men deep for the Spartans.

Epaminondas and Pelopidas were far from the only same-sex couples in Thebes. Philolaus gave laws to the Thebans and he and his lover, the famous Diocles, an Olympic runner and victor, lived together until their deaths. Diocles had been forced to leave his native home, Corinth, due to the incestuous passion of his mother. Male lovers visited their tombs which were side by side but pointed in different directions: Philolaus's pointed towards Thebes and Diocles's towards Corinth.

During one of Epaminondas's incursions into Sparta one of the warriors to take up arms against him was Isadas. The story, very brief, comes from Plutarch and demonstrates the Greek respect for male beauty. Isadas had been home and had oiled himself when he was warned of the Thebans' arrival. He rushed out, as Plutarch say, ''outstanding in both his beauty and his size, a lad between boyhood and adulthood (that Plutarch called boyish), in the bloom of his sweetness, stark naked, bearing only his weapons.'' He helped his fellow Spartans to victory that day and was much applauded by his peers and the ephors, although they found themselves obliged to fine him for not donning protective armor. Thucydides (see Sources) tells us, by the way, that it had been the Spartans who had introduced the oiling of the body with olive oil, and its removal with a strigil.

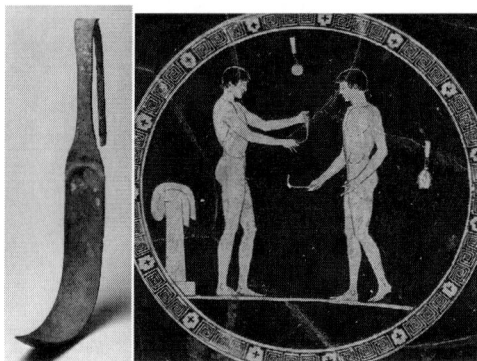

A strigil.

An epigram on a tombstone, concerning the Sacred Band, has been recently found with this inscription: ''Direct your arrows, dear Eros, at these bachelors, that, bold in the love they share they will defend their fatherland, for your arrows fire boldness and of all the gods you, Eros, are supreme at exalting front-line champions.''

Without Epaminondas's leadership Theban hopes for hegemony faded. The Spartans, however, having been again defeated in battle, were unable to replace their losses. The ultimate result of the battle was to pave the way for the rise of Macedonia as the leading force in Greece.

Macedonia had been a Persian possession from the time of Darius (although under the Macedonian king Amyntas I his son Alexander had killed Persian ambassadors demanding earth and water when they became too frisky with Macedonian ladies), and under Xerxes its king Alexander I (Alexander the Great was Alexander III) negotiated alongside the Persian general Mardonius in favor of Persia. In fact Macedonia was little more than a Persian satrap. But Alexander did what he could to warn fellow Greeks of Persian advances, thanks to which the Persians were defeated at Plataea and hounded by Alexander's own troops as they fled from Greece--forever.

Macedonians were considered to be barbarians by Athenians, to the extent that many were refused Athenian schooling. Aristotle himself, for example, a Macedonian, was shunned by all except Plato's Lyceum (4). Macedonians were not even deemed Greek until Elis decided otherwise, allowing them into the Olympic Games of 504 in order to establish their Greekness. Alexander I did what he could to attract poets to his court, two of whom were Pindar (see Sources) and Bacchylides.

The Theban Pindar lived around 500 B.C. and celebrated the Greek victories against the Persians at Salamis and Plataea. His home in Thebes became a must for his devotees. Unlike Xenophon whose prose is so clear that it has been the basis of study by students from the Renaissance to today, Pindar's work is of complex difficulty. Pindar had praised Athens as the bulwark of democracy, a sunlit splendor, for which Thebes, Athens' enemy, fined him 5,000 drachmae, that Athenians reimbursed twofold in gratitude. He was a priest at Delphi, and each night the chair he had occupied when alive was placed outside the doors to the temple so he could dine with the gods, gods he deeply respected in his *oeuvre*. An example of his poetry:

One must pluck love, my dear heart,
In due season, in life's prime.
But whosoever catches with a glance
The rays flashing from Theoxenus' eyes,
And is not tossed on the waves of desire,

Has a black heart forged in cold flame!
But I, like the wax of the sacred bees
When smitten by the sun, melt
When I look at the young limbs of boys.

Macedonians could drink Thracians under the table, something not even Alcibiades had been able to do. The men wore a cord around their waists, a shameful symbol until the kill of their first man allowed them to remove it, and until they had killed a boar they could not sit at the table with other men. There was no lack of Macedonians because the word bacchanalia had been invented for them, although their virile love of boys drained most of the overflow.

Philip of Macedonia was an ardent boy-lover, and had given himself freely when younger. As a boy he was sent to Thebes and placed under the care of the great general Pammenes, another ardent boy-lover, who immediately reserved the young and willing prince for his bed. Years later, when Philip was king of Macedonia, his general Pausanias came to him with the complaint that he had been forcefully sodomized. Pausanias felt that he had the king's ear because they too had been lovers when young. Pausanias claimed that he had had relations with a boy who killed himself when Pausanias threw him over for another. The boy's former lover, a certain Attalus, decided to wreak vengeance on Pausanias by inviting him to a banquet, during which he forcefully raped Pausanias after getting him drunk and tying him up. Pausanias was then violated by Attalus' men and, finally, thrown outside where Attalus' stable boys did the same. Pausanias hoped that King Philip would avenge the outrage by killing Attalus. But Attalus was both an essential general in Philip's army and the father of Philip's wife. So to placate Pausanias, Philip named him to his personal guard, affording Pausanias the proximity he needed to drive a dagger into Philip's chest-- thus opening the way for Philip's son, the Great Alexander.

A slightly different version of this story exists, recounted by Diodorus Siculus. The boy who had committed suicide was Philip II's favorite whom Diodorus says ''was beloved by Philip for his beauty''. The boy committed suicide by stepping in front of Philip during a battle and received the sword thrust meant to kill the king. Attalus had had Pausanias raped multiply times because Pausanias, jealous of the boy, had called him a whore in public. Attalus had tried to gain the boy's love but was refused because the lad chose death due to both Pausanias's insult and the fact that Philip had put him aside for another.

What Philip learned in military terms from Pelopidas, Epaminondas and Pammenes was vital in giving him the credentials needed to be accepted as king, vital in forming a Macedonian army, and the basis for what he taught his son Alexander. Theban techniques that would make him ruler of the world, beginning with the destruction of Thebes itself, a form of the son slaying the father in order to assert his dominance.

Modern historians refuse to even mention Philip's preference for boys, and as far as Alexander is concerned, only one admitted that his closeness to Hephaestion may possibly have had a physical element (16), a distancing from reality that borders on the homophobic, although in their favor Homer never went into the sexuality of Patroclus and Achilles, other than to state that they had a special friendship. Only Plutarch never skirted the subject, stating outright that bonds between certain men and boys like Epaminondas and Pelopidas were stronger than those they felt for others.

To fully understand the above, we can now go into detail, beginning in 368:

During Thebes' rise to power the sons of neighboring kings were sent to Thebes as hostages to ensure the enactment of the treaties between Thebans and those now allied to Thebes. One of these countries was Macedonia who sent 14-year-old Philip there between the years 368 to 365. He learned the art of war under Epaminondas and became the belovèd of Epaminondas's former lover, Pelopidas, as well as that of the Theban general Pammenes with whom he resided. Pammenes himself, when young, had been the belovèd of Epaminondas. (Epaminondas was far from celibate--among his many belovèds was one that stood out for his beauty, Asophichus.)

Philip took the throne of Macedonia in 359 due to the death of his older brothers, Alexander II and Perdiccas III, and after removing Amyntas IV. As this is a fascinating story, I'd like to recount it, although very briefly.

Philip was the son of Amyntas III but he had two older brothers. One was Alexander II

who became king after Amyntas' death. He
provoked Pelopidas of Thebes when he
captured certain parts of Thessaly, which
were Theban reserves. Pelopidas forced
Alexander II to back down and as insurance
of his good faith he made Alexander II hand
over his youngest brother, Philip, who went
directly to Pelopidas's bed before that of
Pammenes. Pelopidas had played a double
role by assuring himself of the backing of
Alexander's brother-in-law Ptolemy. Either
with Pelopidas's consent or not, Ptolemy
killed Alexander and made himself regent
over Alexander's second brother Perdiccas,
judged too young to rule, but not too young to
kill Ptolemy in 365 and take the name of
Perdiccas III. He was called the philosopher
king because he filled his court with followers
of Plato. Perdiccas tried to reconquer some of
the lands Alexander had surrendered, but was
killed in battle. The throne went to Perdiccas'
son Amyntas IV. Just a child, he was at first
tutored by Philip until Philip simple pushed
him aside and took the throne for himself as
Philip II, Alexander the Great's father. He
was genuinely fond of young Amyntas IV and
gave him his own daughter in marriage. As
the boy posed absolutely no threat he lived a

tranquil existence until Philip died and Alexander became king. Judged a *potential* problem, Alexander killed him. Luckily Amyntas hadn't had a son for Alexander to murder, but he did leave a daughter, Eurydice II. Now, after the death of Alexander the Great, Eurydice tried to gain power but was imprisoned by Alexander's mother Olympias who sent her a cup of hemlock, a sword and a noose and told her to choose how she wished to die. She chose the noose. What happened to Olympias will be reported.

Pausanias was one of seven of Philip's bodyguards (the reason why was evoked above) and, taking advantage of Philip being unarmed and unprotected by body armor during the performance of a play, slew him. He then made a dash for it to coconspirators waiting for him with his horse outside. He is said to have tripped over a vine and was hacked to death by three of Philip's other guards, mad with anger because Philip had been greatly loved.

The Latin historian Justin (see Sources) states that Alexander's mother Olympias was in on the plot, the proof being that after his death she placed a crown on Pausanias corpse and ordered annual sacrifices to him until her own death. Modern historians doubt both the story of the homosexual motive for Pausanias's revenge and the possibility that Olympias would have dared tried anything against a king as revered by his men as had been Philip, which is probably true. Concerning Pausanias, later homophobia taints any evaluation of what took place and, anyway, at a distance of nearly 2,500 years any assertions at all make as much sense at spitting against the wind. Concerning Olympias, Justin lived perhaps 500 years later (we don't know exactly) so we'll never ever know if she placed a crown on the body or his grave or anything else about their complotting together. Amusingly, one historian states that Pausanias's decision to kill Philip because he'd been raped wasn't sufficient motivation, as if any man could live with the memory and the physical pain and disgust of such an outrage, homosexual or not, without murder in his heart.

Pausanias's three sons, in the blind injustice of the times, were butchered.

Philip comes to our attention as king during the Third Sacred War (356 – 346). All three wars were centered around the Delphic

Amphictyonic League (Amphictyonic meaning neighbors; an obscure and incredibly long-lasting league formed after the Trojan War and consisting of Boeotians, Dorians, Ionians, Locrians, Phocians, Thessalians, among twenty others during this period). The Amphictyonic League came to the aid of Delphi when the nearby town of Krissa imposed a tax on those seeking to cross its territory in search of oracles. This started the First Sacred War, which led to the destruction of Krissa. The Second Sacred War was set off when Phocis tried to take possession of the sacred shrine. Sparta intervened and Phocis withdrew.

The Third Sacred War began when Phocis was fined for cultivating sacred land. In retaliation the Phocians seized Delphi again, located in the valley of Phocis, and its immeasurable treasury, so vast that the Phocians could now buy armies to fight off those who opposed their takeover of the imminently sacred site, especially their nearby enemies Thebes and Thessaly. The war wore out the participants to such an extent that they appealed to Philip II of Macedonia, who was biding his time for just such an event. Phocis, despite the incredible sacrilege, was morally supported by many members of the League because they felt that the Leagues' dominant leader, Thebes, had fined Phocians far too much in the beginning in hopes they would rebel, offering Thebes the occasion to take control of Phocis.

Delphi was a part of Phocis, the darkest shade.

As member state after member state raised an army against Phocis, despite their sympathy for them, Phocians used their new army to nip the danger in the bud, winning battle after battle except for one they lost against Pammenes, the ardent boy-lover who had bedded Philip II of Macedonia when he was a lad. For unknown reasons Pammenes didn't follow through on his victory and destroy Phocis.

In one battle where the Phocians were in a tight position the Phocian commander, Onomarchus, ordered the Phocian citizens to leave their city--the old, women and children-- and stand before the walls while he bolted the city gates behind them. The army confronting them, in this case the Sacred Band led by Pelopidas, immediately understanding that the Phocians were prepared to fight to the last child, withdrew.

The Phocians reinforced their troops and entered Thessaly to do preventive battle against Philip of Macedonia who was there to aid the Thessalians. As the Phocians had acquired catapults they did so much damage Philip lost his first two battles, withdrawing after making the declaration of a true leader: ''Like a ram I pull back to butt again harder.'' The Thessalians, underawed by Philip's showing so far, nonetheless put their forces under his orders. Philip then met the Phocians in battle near Pagasae, his men crowned in Apollo's laurels as they were there to free Delphi. As the poet wrote: ''Delphi. In the beginning the gods freed two high-flying eagles, one from the East, the other from the West. They met on the lofty crags of a great mountain that loomed over a jagged valley and the far-off port of Cirrha. Here was the sacred center of the universe; here was the spiritual navel of the Hellenes; here was Delphi, home of Apollo. For Apollo had left his birthplace on Cycladic Delos to teach Man wisdom by revealing to him the future. Apollo traveled to the heights of Mount Parnassus where he destroyed the snake-like dragon, Python, its guardian. Then, with the help of the Muses and the consent of Mother Earth, he recruited sailors from a passing Cretan ship whom he made priests, and irreproachable villagers from the nearby village of Krissa whom he ordained priestesses, sometimes called Pythonesses in memory of the dragon. He built a temple, initiated the love of the arts, taught moderation and humaneness in all things, and himself tried to exemplify the virtuous life.'' (3)

Now the Thessalians and Macedonians entered in battle against the Phocians in what Herodotus says was the bloodiest in history until then. 6,000 Phocians were butchered on the battlefield and 3,000 taken prisoner, later drowned at Delphi's demand, the price paid by temple robbers, as drowning deprived them of burial.

Thessaly made Philip their Archon (meaning both leader and lord) for life, the very foundation of the power that would be his and his son's. Phocis, certain that Philip would now enter their territory and destroy them, appealed to Athens and Sparta for help, both of whom had no choice but to rally behind the Phocians as a way of protecting themselves from Philip who now, in addition to Thessaly, had the backing of Thebans. The Athenians forbade him to send troops through Thermopylae, the gateway to Phocis and the entrance to Attica, fearing that Philip would seize Athens too.

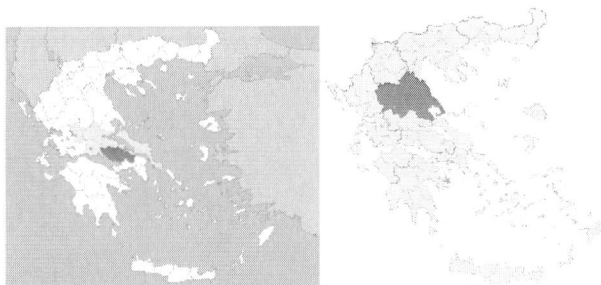

Thebes in Boeotia, darkest shade on the left,
Thessaly is the darker shade on the right.

So Philip ordered a conference, the purpose of which was to draw up a treaty that would prevent war between Athens, Sparta, Macedonia and Macedonia's allies. Once he had the Athenians at the peace table, he drew out making a decision until his troops had had time to descend and occupy Thermopylae. Thusly exposed, the Athenians could only sign a treaty that would protect themselves from Philip's army. Phocis was taken, but instead of being totally destroyed as requested by Delphi, only the towns were torn down and the inhabitants resettled in settlements never to grow over 50 houses. The money the Phocians had stolen was to be reimbursed at 60 talents a year. The Phocian commander Onomarchus had been killed during the fighting but Philip had the body brought to him and crucified, and then denied it burial. Macedonia was admitted into the Delphic Amphictyonic League, a symbolic declaration that it was no longer considered a barbarian leper.

Philip set to work building up an army, taking his time so as not to incite his neighbors to league together against him. The localities he seized were where gold could be found, *le nerd de la guerre*. Some places he took and then handed over as goodwill gifts to those he wished to have as friends; some leaders he needed he simply bribed, perhaps surprising himself by what a little gold or loot could buy. He welded together, for the first time, the different peoples who made up Macedonia, especially those of the coast and those in the mountains, savage and treacherous even when they were not drinking.

Philip surrounded himself with Royal Pages, the sons of nobles and chieftains whom he trained as bodyguards and, later, officials, who were hostages that guaranteed their fathers' obeisance, and were, as a matter of course, sexually available. There were 200 of them, aged 14 to 18. They were extremely well treated and well educated. A later generation of Pages would revolt against Philip's son Alexander and be slain to the last.

Macedonia

Later Philip, like his son Alexander, would treat Athens with kid gloves, even though Athens, under the rhetoric of Demosthenes, accused Philip of every evil under the sun; even though Athenians considered Macedonians little more evolved than baboons; and even though Athens repeatedly sent armies and ships against Philip, even if Philip defeated them every time. The question is Why? The answer could only come from the three years Philip had been obliged to reside in Thebes as a hostage under Epaminondas, Pelopidas and Pammenes, years seemingly vital in the military techniques he acquired, but something must have gone monstrously wrong. Perhaps he had not been shown enough respect; perhaps he had been sexually abused--the fact that he was attracted to men would in no way have excused something so heinous as rape. Or perhaps he felt that Thebes, the conqueror of Sparta, was the power he would eventually be called upon to defeat, this *despite* his *perhaps* having been well received and well cared for when he was a boy hostage.

As the British were to do in the 1800s in England, he recruited men that he allowed to be trained where they lived, alongside the boys they'd grown up with, who shared the same accent, or even the same dialect, so diverse were they. He gave them cloaks in place of skins, turned them from fighting among themselves to fighting barbarians and seizing their wealth, to become civilized, thanks to obedience to Philip's laws. Then he organized gatherings where the men would live among their own but train intermixed, until they became used to the others, at which moment he introduced a new word for them all: Macedonia, of which they were members, under a unique banner, the Vergina Sun.

In unifying Macedonia Philip used every tool and persuasion open to him, and I mean *every*: To avoid unrest in a western region, Epirus, he had the king send his son, age 12, to Philip's court at Pella. There, wrote Justin (Sources): ''He made every effort to seduce the boy, pretending to love him, entering into a homosexual union with the boy, his motive being to gain the boy's submission, making him first his catamite and then a king.'' Later the boy married Philip's daughter Cleopatra and gave Philip his sister, Olympias. Although Philip would have seven wives, he had but two sons, Alexander the Great and another boy mentally unstable.

Justin tells us that Philip moved entire populations from one part of his kingdom to another, according to his judgment that one place needed more inhabitants, that another had too many. So afraid were those ordered about that none dared even shed tears, but just ''looked with yearning at the tombs of the ancestors that they were abandoning''.

Philip decided to end revolts in northern Macedonia, an area known as the Chalcidice, a kind of three-pronged peninsula where Aristotle had been born. The area had a singularity: it had given sanctuary to two of Philip's half-brothers, a third, Archelaus, Philip is said to have murdered on taking the throne. Philip ravaged the towns in the Chalcidice, slaughtered the men, including his two half-brothers, and enslaved the women and children, a lesson to those who would oppose him.

Philip introduced a system of rewards, giving men money for extra-valiant bravery, or advancement into his Companions, a post sought by all, or grants of land.

Until then the poorly armed troops that could not afford complete armor were called peltasts. These became of prime importance to Philip and, later, Alexander, because they were maneuverable. The phalanx, a metal porcupine, was reinforced with huge spears called *sarissa*, up to 18 feet (5.5 meters) long. The cavalry could move their horses thanks to directions given by their knees, but they were nonetheless hampered by the lack of stirrups, not as yet invented. Philip constantly drilled his men, and where other armies had one servant per man, Philip allowed one in ten, meaning the men had to carry their own package. He also bawled out a soldier who bathed in warm water, reserved for women.

As for a fleet, Philip and Alexander's huge gamble was that they could win without a full navy, and although both had ships, they did not overly depend on them, a risk that paid off at the end of Alexander's oriental adventure when he freed himself of all but 20 vessels.

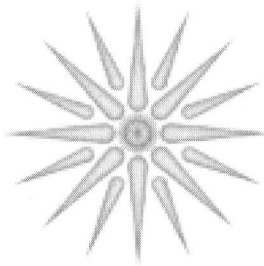

Vergina Sun.

From childhood the Spartans had embraced the notion of service to their state; for the Macedonians all was new. But they adapted easily thanks to the wealth that would soon be theirs, the new lands they would seize, the adventure, and the hundreds of throats they would slit. There was no greater excitation than the act of killing and the scent of blood that would drive them to the limits of their sanity, engorging their muscles, for the thrill of taking a life was more intoxicating than any alcohol, the shock of the swords against leather armor, the piercing thrust and wild-eyed surprise of he who felt it enter him, transpierce him, the eyes glazed before turning up into the skull, the broken body falling free of the sword that had taken his life, so precious to him, of such indifference to men and gods.

**I deeply regret that this magnificent gold casket,
wherein rest Philip's cremated bones and ashes, is not in color.**

At banquets they would toast each other, all regions united, all men with the same aim, all Macedonians, the world their oyster. Lying alongside one another on couches, drunk from wine and the promise of the future, they would caress and kiss openly, guffaw and whoop, their hands pleasing the man in front, hands lost in tunics, heads bent back while tongues entwined, and the moans of those entered from behind.

All of which is eternal. All of which will eternally be.

Under Alexander the orgies would become more unbridled still, part of the reason why the men, who shared immense equality with their king, could not accept prostrating themselves to him when he took on Persian pretentions, not when, to not put too fine a point on it, they had had their cocks up him and his up them.

Philip perfected his strategy. The time-honored tactic was no longer the phalanx, although the phalanx was still essential, but now it was looser, giving the men freer play. It served to hold the adversary in place, while the cavalry descended to wreak havoc, havoc Spartans would never be victim to because neither Philip nor his son would ever attack the city, nor feel, between their toes, the grass alongside the Eurotas River, at the foot of the Taygetus Mountains. Philip did threaten the Spartans, though, sending this message: ''You are advised to surrender immediately for if I bring my armies into your land I will destroy your farms, slay your people and raze your city!''

The Spartans' laconic response: ''*If.*''

Philip's preparations for war took place hidden among the hills, that no outsider knew even existed. Philip's marriage to Olympias went unheralded. The birth a year later of a son went unnoticed.

The destruction of Thebes began when Philip asked the Thebans permission to cross their territory to attack Athens, Philip having had enough of Demosthenes and Athenians putting up obstacles each time he made a move. To sweeten the deal, Philip promised to give Thebes all the loot the Macedonians would eventually steal from Athens. Thebes was glad to agree, especially as this would eliminate Athens as a potential obstacle to Theban ascension.

Athens sent Demosthenes to Thebes to convince the Thebans to remain loyal to Athens, and against all expectations they agreed, although they demanded to be placed commanders over the Athenian troops and the Athenian navy that would be called up, along with Theban troops, to fight Philip. Demosthenes' speech was said to have played a decisive role in convincing the Thebans to forgo the looting of Athens, but we shall never know as there is no record of what he said. Athens could count on little help from surrounding states, quite simply because everyone had been fed up with Athenian grandeur and arrogance. Since the city's founding by Athena, Athens had exploited its neighbors, especially in the Delian League, making them pay for Athens' wondrous buildings, Long Walls and navy, and that for two centuries. Nearly everyone remained neutral except for little Phocis, the cause of the Sacred Wars, who hated Thebes because the Thebans had wanted to reduce the country to ashes, and were grateful to Philip for leaving them their lives (although 9,000 Phocians had nonetheless perished).

Athenians and Thebans met Philip's troops in battle at Chaeronea, a plain near both Phocis and Thebes. ''If the Greeks won they would retain their freedom and autonomy. If Philip won, Greece was his. It was as simple as that,'' wrote Ian Worthington in his book *Philip II of Macedonia*. Meaning the end to Greek liberty.

Philip had 30,000 men and 2,000 horse; Athens and Thebes 30,000 men and 3,800 horse.

For such a vital battle we know incredibly little, in fact nearly nothing. Worthington tells us that Philip sized up the enemy's strategy instantly, an ''instinct ... Alexander inherited and would use time and again.''

From the very founding of Macedonia, Philip had untiringly trained his men, as

Alexander would also do (as Frederick the Great would do too, taking command of the training himself, spotting the boys who would share his tent for the night).

The allies had nothing of Philip's troops' discipline and nearly immediately folded, except for the Sacred Band that fought on until not a single lover and his belovèd remained alive. Alexander, just 18, was there too, and it was he Philip had put in command of the men who annihilated those so carefully chosen and nurtured by Epaminondas and Pelopidas.

Philip is said to have searched the battlefield for the Sacred Band, and to have burst into tears on finding the remains. He erected a Lion on the spot, and raised a mound seven meters high over his own Macedonians, both shrines visible today to those of us lucky enough to pay homage to the green fields of Marathon, Thermopylae and Chaeronea, to place a foot on the hallowed land of immortal Greece, the father of us all.

Another view of the Lion of Chaeronea, restored by the Order of Chaeronea, a secret, quasi-Masonic society of homosexuals.

It is with the destruction of Thebes that our history of the Sacred Band, massacred to the last belovèd, comes to an end. But we must bring the story full circle with the death of the young god Alexander, a god sacralized by the Greeks, the Persians and the Egyptians--a god dead as has died, sooner or later, every god and/or gods invented by the fertile and ever-fearful minds of humans--at the ungodly age of 32.

We continue with the relationship between Alexander the Great and Hephaestion, while recounting the life of Aristotle, their teacher. Aristotle was born in the town of Stagira, to the far north of Greece, in a kind of three-tentacled peninsula called Chalcidice. His father was a physician which should have been Aristotle's career too, as being a physician in Greece at the time was a heritage handed down from father to son. But he died when Aristotle was ten, the same age that Alcibiades lost his father, and like Alcibiades, Aristotle was of the nobility and well off financially.

Alexander and Hephaestion.

At the time the region was under the thumb of the Macedonian king Amyntas III. Very exceptionally Amyntas lived to the ripe old age of 80, an exception in a country nearly as savage as Thrace, where sons, uncles, nephews and brothers killed each other off with what seemed to be innate talent. I went into the lives of the progeny of Amyntas in the section on Philip, so suffice it to say that three of Amyntas' sons eventually became king: Alexander II, Perdiccas II and Philip II, father of the Great Alexander (III). Philip reigned an impressive 23 years. The line of Amyntas III would end with Alexander the Great, who would also be the last Persian emperor.

We know that Aristotle had at least one brother, unnamed, who produced a son, Callisthenes, who, thanks to Aristotle, became Alexander's historian. But when he refused to prostrate himself before Alexander in the Persian manner, Alexander had him tortured under the suspicion of fomenting a revolt, and put to death.

At age 17 Aristotle went to Athens, a huge city of 150,000, other city-states in Greece having populations that rarely exceeded 40,000. As war was an Athenian constant, Aristotle estimated that 2,000 Athenians a year died in battle.

Alexander's father Philip II.

There were two great schools at the time of Aristotle's arrival, that of Isocrates and that of Plato. Isocrates' school was based on rhetoric, training for public speakers and lawyers, a sure guarantee of wealth. Speakers in Athens were highly praised and often elected to important positions. Every educated Greek was expected to speak convincingly, whatever the subject, and could win prizes of considerable value. Isocrates was rich thanks to his father who manufactured flutes and, like his father, he had a good head for business, charging his pupils 1,000 drachmae, a huge sum. Plato's school was more liberal, and it was there that Aristotle chose to go, perhaps in part because Plato accepted

Macedonians more readily, a people that most Athenians found coarse and domineering. Courses were free for those who couldn't pay. Plato had been an accomplished athlete in his youth, trained in gymnastics. He gave up an athletic career when he heard Socrates speak. Plato is known to have loved a certain Aster, meaning ''star''. He wrote, ''You gaze at the stars, my Star; were I Heaven so that I could gaze at you with many eyes.'' He also loved Agathon, described as the handsomest boy in Athens: ''When I kiss Agathon my soul is on my lips.'' Plato's classes took place in the Academy, land left to him by a man named Academus. It contained statues and sepulchers, plane trees and olive groves, and, eventually, Plato's tomb. The school would go on for 900 years.

Alexander

In 343 B.C. Philip II invited Aristotle to his court to give instruction to Alexander, age 13, and his inseparable companion Hephaestion (16). Worthington wrote that Philip sent Alexander to Mieza ''to be better able to concentrate on his studies, and hence sent him away to a 'boarding school'.'' Aristotle considered Hephaestion a far more assiduous student than Alexander and noted that Alexander shared all his secrets with the boy who was ''by far his dearest friend''. As they were the same age they most probably shared each other's bodies in equal measure, neither one being predominantly the lover or the belovèd. Athenaeus (see Sources) says that Alexander ''had a boundless passion for beautiful boys''. He, Hephaestion and their friends certainly practiced sex from the very onset of puberty, an act as prevalent and shared as boys pissing side-by-side. In addition to mutual fondling, they moved on, as did all Greek boys in the total absence of girls, to sex that was largely intercrural, one of the boys lying on his stomach or leaning against a wall while the other entered his closed thighs from behind, kissing his ears and neck and reaching around to give pleasure to his friend's manhood. All other forms of physical release were assuredly, at times, present. Their friendship was compared--by their friends--as resembling that between Achilles and Patroclus (3). Sex was a vital aspect of Greek life, and Arrian claims that Alexander himself said: "Sex and sleep alone make me conscious that I am mortal."

As noted earlier, Greek boys were raised by their mothers, which predisposed them to favor men, since such was a woman's preference. In Alexander's case this was enhanced by a mother who took him into her bed, certainly not incestuously but as a way of cementing their relationship, especially as she knew he was destined, by nature, to follow his father to the throne. She was superstitious and he became exceedingly so. She inspired him with stories of the great men who had preceded him, and assured him of his ability and destiny in assuming his future kingship. She must also have been hard because later, when Alexander captured Darius's mother, sisters and daughters, he became very close to them all, even marrying one of the daughters, and told them that his mother Olympias was the kind of woman who charged him rent for the nine months she housed him in her womb.

She worshipped snakes, presumably because one, in the form of Zeus, had entered her womb through the passage reserved for her husband, and deposited Alexander. At the same time his father was absent, in winter and summer, on campaigns. An absent father and all-invasive mother combined to form a perfect compost for seeding same-sex desire. Philip recognized his boy's ability, naming him regent during one of his absences when Alexander was only 16, and appointing him head of Philip's own all-important Companion Cavalry at age 18. This turned out to be vital as it was the army, through acclamation, that decided who would rule Macedonia.

Philip turned over the shrine of the Nymphs at Mieza as a study room for the boys and their companions, and in thanks for Aristotle's services he rebuilt Aristotle's hometown of Stagira that he had previously destroyed when the town offered resistance to his army. Of huge importance is the fact that Aristotle's father, Nicomachus, had been the personal physician of Philip II's father Amyntas III.

A moving story recounted by Aristotle concerns an uncontrollable horse that the boy

Alexander managed to break in, the legendary Bucephalas (Alexander's companion for thirty years). When he jumped down his father, an incredibly harsh man, went to him shedding tears, kissed him and told him to find a kingdom worthy of him, as Macedonia was far too small. Aristotle taught him the art of medicine as he himself had been instructed before his father's early death, instruction that continued afterwards thanks to other members of his family who wanted to see Aristotle follow in his father's steps. Alexander always carried a copy of Homer's *Iliad* that he kept under his pillow, annotated by Aristotle, with his dagger. Dionysius of Halicarnassus informs us that Alexander, Hephaestion and their companions were Aristotle's pupils for eight years. Aristotle may have lost prestige when, later, his nephew Callisthenes turned on Alexander and was executed. Plutarch seems to confirm this possibility, saying that when Aristotle arrived Alexander loved him as much as he did his own father, "for his father gave him life while Aristotle taught him how to live life." But then things changed and Alexander only remained with Aristotle because of his unquenchable thirst for knowledge. One has the impression that Alexander's mind was incredibly mobile, flashing from one philosophy to another, shifting from tutor to tutor, idea to idea, as he did sexually from boy to boy, although Hephaestion was most assuredly the love of his life, especially as Hephaestion was always, irrevocably, his staunchest pillar.

Alexander and Hephaestion formed a partnership during which Hephaestion commanded troops, built bridges, went on diplomatic missions, founded new settlements, as well as performing the incredible multitude of other tasks necessary when one rode with Alexander. During the siege of Tyre Alexander turned over the fleet to him, a difficult enterprise as the men he commanded had been conquered by Alexander's army and were thusly not the most responsive of allies.

Alexander

When Hephaestion died from fever in Ecbatana at age 32, Alexander was prostrated with grief. He sent to the Oracle at Siwa to ask if he could deify his lover. The Oracle allowed him to make Hephaestion a divine hero, which seems to have satisfied him. At the time of his own death, a year later, Alexander was still making plans for the monuments, cities and shrines to be erected in his companion's honor, as Hadrian would later do for Antinous (17).

Hephaestion had been sent to Athens to work out a reconciliation with Demosthenes, an orator of immense importance who had first opposed the military advances of Philip II, and then those of Alexander himself. Known for his love of boys, it's not impossible that this was a reason why Alexander dispatched the handsome Hephaestion. History's judgment of Demosthenes is unsavory. He had inherited great wealth and surrounded himself with youths, Aristion, Cnosion, Moschus, Aristarchus, to name a very few, whom he prostituted to augment his income. Demosthenes was thought to have been sexually passive, a highly disrespected role for a man in Athens where the act was reserved for boys, the penetrated always considered to be either a youth or someone unacceptably effeminate, which was Demosthenes' case. To gain the favors of noble youths, Demosthenes did not hesitate to promise them ascendance over Athenians, thanks to the oratorical skills they would learn from him, an ancient casting couch. Once he gained control over a wealthy boy he would do what he could to despoil him.

Demosthenes was guilty of breaking two Athenian laws. The first stated that any Athenian who prostituted himself, and then made himself known in a public sense (speaking before the Assembly, for example) could be stoned to death. The second law had a similar penalty for those who showed hubris. As Dover says, ''Hubris is a term applied to any kind of behavior in which one treats other people just as one pleases, with an arrogant confidence that one will escape paying any penalty for violating their rights and disobeying any law or moral rule accepted by society.'' Both Demosthenes and Alcibiades were multiple offenders of the law, but both were protected in high places.

Demosthenes was the son of a sword-maker who died when the boy was seven, leaving him a fortune that was embezzled to such an extent that he could afford only minor tutors, robbing him of a first-class education. Whether due to this or other reasons, the boy grew to be spiteful and received the name snake. Extremely weak and sickly, he encountered his destiny at a very young age when he was literally smuggled into court where he heard the orator Callistratus, and recognized that declaiming would be his life ambition. It's uncertain who taught him rhetoric, but he hadn't enough money to pay Isocratus although in one way or another he succeeded in mastering the skills taught by Isocratus, Plato, Isaeus and others.

He used his knowledge to bring his guardians to trial in an attempt to recuperate what they had stolen, and succeeded in regaining a fraction. At the same time, following doctors' orders, he tried to build up his strength through running and exercise, even winning some races. He turned to pleading as a profession but Plutarch tells us his voice was weak and unpleasant, his manner vulgar, he was short to breath (bizarre for a runner) and broke up his sentences in such a way as to make them incomprehensible.

He then came upon the actor Satyrus who had him declaim from Euripides before halting him and then teaching the correct way. Demosthenes went on to practice for months, going so far as to shave half his head so that he would not be tempted to go outside. He declaimed with pebbles in his mouth, at times running up and down stairs, other times in front of mirrors. The practice paid off to the extent that one lawyer, seeing him rise, said out loud, ''Here comes the knife that will destroy my plea,'' Plutarch tells us.

Despite the fear Philip II raised with his victories, Demosthenes persuaded, through the eloquence of his rhetoric, both the Athenians and the Thebans to do the right thing by uniting against future Macedonian conquests, ''as Pericles would have done in

Athens, were he still alive,'' said Demosthenes, ''and Epaminondas would have done in Thebes.'' His discourse infuriated King Philip and the boy at his side, Alexander. Yet for all his crowing, in the next battle, that at Thermodon, Demosthenes was the first to cast away his shield and run for his life, to Philip's glee. Philip, said by Plutarch to have been drunk, wandered through the bodies of the thousands of dead strewn over the battlefield, claiming it the work of Demosthenes and his oratory. The Persians, however, impressed by Demosthenes' tongue and his ability to move Athenians and Thebans to action, showered him with money.

As a boy Demosthenes had been called Batalos, batalos with two t's meaning stammerer (which he was), with one t meaning someone who likes to be taken anally, the origin of which comes from an effeminate aulos player, Batalos.

Batalos playing his aulos.

When Philip was assassinated Demosthenes offered up public thanks to the gods and tried to convince Athenians to fight on the side of the countries who revolted when the death became known. But when the Athenians saw with what incredible rapidity and savagery his son Alexander the Great took things in hand, they sent a delegation to plead for his forgiveness, a plea that Alexander acquiesced to.

Shortly afterwards a boyhood friend of Alexander, Harpalus, asked for sanctuary in Athens after stealing a great deal of money. In fact, this was the third time he had fled from Macedonia with funds that were not his own, but as Harpalus had been a close companion (and was, in fact, Alexander's Treasurer), Alexander had always forgiven him. The

Athenians granted him asylum, and the money he came to Athens with was put in Demosthenes' care. Of the 700 talents, a fabulous sum, 350 disappeared. (Other sources state that it was 1,500 talents that the Athenians recuperated in its entirety and later used in wars against Macedonia.) While an enquiry went on, Harpalus fled to Crete and Demosthenes took the first boat to Aegina. Demosthenes was found guilty but the Athenians felt he was of such importance--thanks to his rhetorical skills and counsel--that a ship was sent to bring him home.

It was at this moment that Hephaestion arrived in Athens to work out a settlement. Demosthenes' answer was to spread the rumor that Alexander, on campaign in Thrace, had been killed, as had his entire army. Hephaestion rushed to Thrace where he found his friend and his army intact. Furious, Alexander marched towards Athens, demanding along the way that the city hand over eight of its orators, among them Demosthenes. Demosthenes told the Assembly the story of the sheep that had handed over their dogs to the wolves, and the inevitable result. A delegation caught up with Alexander and, again, begged forgiveness.

It was accorded, but following the death of Alexander the Macedonians ordered his capture. Demosthenes preferred poison to being tortured and executed by Alexander's men, poison he kept, says Eratosthenes (see Sources on this exceptional man), in a ring on his finger. Thusly ended the life of this repugnant, albeit brilliant, personage.

The murder of Harpalus is unclear. He crossed over to Crete and was assassinated by his servant, whether for the servant's personal gain or because he had been ordered to do so is a mystery. As we see elsewhere, Alexander could be cruelly vindictive, but Harpalus, lame, had shared Alexander's boyhood, and later he sent Alexander everything he could find in literature, especially Aeschylus, Sophocles, Euripides, Philoxenus, Telestes and others. So why he was finally dispatched is unknown.

Plutarch ends the life of Demosthenes with this charming anecdote: a soldier, summoned by his officer to explain himself on some unknown accusation, placed what he had in gold in the hands of Demosthenes' statue, as a request for Demosthenes to give him eloquence. A wind is said to have covered Demosthenes' hands with leaves, so that when the boy returned, having been acquitted, he found his gold intact. He told his story and soon all Athens knew about the restitution of the soldier's gold and what it implied--that Demosthenes had been an honest man all along.

Parmenion was a great general under Philip, responsible for many victories and at times was used as an ambassador. Alexander was deeply in Parmenion's debt when he put General Attalus to death because Attalus opposed Alexander's ascension to the throne after his father Philip's assassination. Attalus's niece, Cleopatra, was Philip's 7th wife, and Attalus hoped Philip would produce a legitimate heir to the throne because Olympias, Philip's 4th wife and Alexander's mother, was Greek and Cleopatra Macedonian. On Philip's death Alexander had not only Attalus murdered, but also Cleopatra and her children by Philip, although other sources claim she committed suicide when she came upon her children's dead bodies. An exclusively homosexual quadrangle had ended the lives of Philip, Pausanias and now Attalus, along with the boy who had killed himself because Pausanias loved another, a death

Attalus had avenged, because he had loved the boy in question, by raping Pausanias.

During a drunken argument in which Alexander felt insulted by Attalus, he had asked his father to put Attalus in his place, which Philip refused to do. When Alexander then insulted Philip, the king came at him with his sword but tripped over a table and fell. ''This is the man,'' scoffed Alexander, ''who wants to cross over to Persia, but can't even cross a room.'' Due to this incident Philip exiled Alexander's closest, most intimate friends but, tellingly, not Hephaestion, perhaps because he knew he would lose his boy for good.

Before his death Attalus had tried to worm his way back into Alexander's favor by turning over letters he had received from the Athenian Demosthenes, letters that promised Athenian support should Attalus kill Alexander. Alas, this hadn't been enough to save him.

Numerous relations of Parmenion were named to key positions, even his lover Amyntas, and his son Philotas, were put in charge of Alexander's Companion Cavalry, his personal bodyguard, a hugely important and honorable post. Parmenion had been

Philip's second in command and remained so under Alexander.

Parmenion dampened Alexander's exuberance and his quest for new tactics, Arrian (see Sources) and Diodorus Siculus maintaining that he saved Alexander, time and again, from defeat and possible death, thanks to his tried strategies and calming presence, while others insist that Alexander basically did what he thought best, with little regard for Parmenion. We have this exchange between the two men: When Darius sent envoys offering peace Parmenion said, ''I would accept it if I were Alexander. ''As would I,'' answered Alexander, ''were I Parmenion.''

Parmenion's son was accused of plotting Alexander's death. Known for his arrogance, he was one of many who despised kowtowing to Alexander once he'd crowned himself King of Persia. He was tortured under the direction of Hephaestion, who took his place as chief Companion, and was then stoned or speared to death, versions vary.

As his father Parmenion was of immense influence, as stated, with members of his family and his friends in every key part of Alexander's entourage, government and armed forces, he had to be killed too, which Alexander did by immediately expediting two of his most faithful intimates, Cleandor and Sitalces, who took no chances with the old warrior, both stabbing him when he was unarmed. Parmenion could not have known the reason, and perhaps had had time to ask his assassins, ''Why, why, why!?!''

At the end of the Sacred Wars Thebes and Athens, pushed on by the effective rhetoric of Demosthenes, decided to go to war with Philip. Philip needed no prompting to send his troops into Boeotia, in 338, to confront and to rout the enemy in the Battle of Chaeronea, the actual unrolling of which is completely unknown. This ended Greek democracies, because afterwards tyrants, monarchies and oligarchies held sway. Philip was now the undisputed leader of Greece, with the exception of Sparta.

I'm going to put in another battle here, that took place immediately after Alexander's death, because historians believe that it too put a nail in the coffin of Greek democracy. As will be reported in detail in a moment, Antipater was placed as regent over the as yet unborn Alexander IV. Thebes and Athens--

thanks in part to the 1,500 talents Harpalus had stolen from Alexander, and Athens had stolen from him--rose up to free themselves of Macedonian hegemony. The battle that then took place, called both the Lamian and the Hellenic War (323-322) started off well for the democrats until the Macedonians were reinforced by Persians, after which they were submerged in a tidal wave. It was after this battle that Demosthenes was forced to commit suicide.

Philip and his new allies formed the League of Corinth that would be the basis for his ascension and that of his son, until Alexander disbanded it when he had enough Greek troops, so many in fact that he would eventually send 10,000 home, replaced by his new Persian boys.

At the moment of Philip's own assassination, in 336, Thebes revolted on the news. But Macedonian troops were already garrisoned on the Cadmea, to which Alexander sent reinforcements. The revolt was put down without major consequences. In 335, however, on the false rumor of Alexander's death in battle, Thebes revolted again, abetted by Athens under the impulse of Demosthenes. Two weeks later Alexander was before the walls of the city but the democratic government of Thebes, although shocked by the rapidity of Alexander's reaction, voted to resist, to Alexander's utter surprise and fury, certain the Thebans were showing disrespect due to his youth (21 at the time). Diodorus claims the Thebans read a proclamation stating that not only were they fighting for democracy, but they went so far as to invite those among Alexander's men who thirsted for freedom to join them.

Alexander, enraged, decided to make an example of Thebes by destroying it utterly, leaving in place only its temples and Pindar's home. How utterly we do not know, but can only hope the boys were spared, to be enrolled later in Alexander's army. The girls and women who survived were certainly sold into slavery. We can only hope, also, that the men died in combat and not by crucifixion, a form of agonizing death that Alexander seemed to have been predisposed to. It was true that many Greeks wanted Thebes punished for having medized, and so looked on Thebes' punishment as being deserved, but in this Macedonia had been equally guilty.

Hephaestion was appointed, along with

Cleitus, joint commanders of Alexander's personal guard, the Companion Cavalry. Hephaestion was in agreement with his lover that the Macedonians and Persians should integrate. Indeed, he was Alexander's torchbearer--his best man--when Alexander married Roxana. Cleitus and the older guard were against Alexander's adoption of Persian ways. It was because Aristotle's nephew, Callesthenes, refused to grovel to Alexander that he was now killed.

Callisthenes was the son of Aristotle's niece, as reported, and as such Alexander took him on as his historian. At first full of praise for Alexander, he later joined Alexander's men in criticizing Alexander's attempts to Persianize the Macedonians, making them marry Persian women and wear Persian dress. On the trumped-up charge of treason he was, according to Ptolemy, crucified, or, according to Aristobulus, imprisoned, where he became lice-ridden and died of disease and neglect. Justin claims that, after the Persian custom, his nose and ears were cut off and he was put in a cage like a dog until one of Alexander's bodyguards took pity of him and put poison in his food. His good Athenian friend Theophrastus wrote *Treatise on Grief* in his memory, and what we know of Callisthenes' writings comes through early historians who took notes before all was lost.

Just as Philip had been killed by Pausanias, so to, apparently, a Page planned to kill Alexander in revenge for Alexander's having punished him when, during a hunt-- one of Alexander's passions--the boy had killed a boar that he should have left, due to Macedonian protocol, to Alexander, states Paul Cartledge. Callisthenes' name was linked to the Pages (the Page had enrolled friends), and the Pages were tortured and hanged. (We know nothing about the exact role Callisthenes may have played.)

Alexander had a history of extreme violence:

In 335 he destroyed Thebes utterly.

He murdered his greatest general Parmenion and Parmenion's son Philotas. He then put their assassins (who had followed Alexander's orders) to death five years later.

He tortured and hanged his historian Callisthenes because he refused to prostrate himself at Alexander's feet in the Persian way.

He had Batis, the governor of Tyre, dragged behind a chariot around the city walls, as Achilles had dragged the body of

Hector--only Hector had been dead, while Batis was alive. He then had 2,000 Tyrians crucified, cruel payment for having made him siege the city for seven months.

When forced to leave India because his men refused to continue on due to monsoon rains, homesickness, disease, injuries and wounds during battles, he retreated while massacring the populations of every village he came across, to vent his anger. He brought his men back to Persia in 326 through the Gedrosian Desert, causing the death of thousands from heat, exhaustion and thirst.

Once back in Persia he cashiered 10,000 and ordered them home.

He destroyed Persepolis as well. Persepolis was built by Darius and enhanced by Xerxes, a treasure in itself, one filled with works of art and literature. Diodorus Siculus states that Alexander allowed his men to sack the surrounding towns after slaughtering all the men, stealing enough gold and jewels to make them wealthy for life, before assuaging their lust on the surviving women.

Alexander reserved Persepolis for himself, making away with 2,500 tons of gold and silver on mules and 3,000 camels. Although he would later be the first to medize--adopting Persian dress and customs--at the time of his first conquests he wanted only revenge against those who had twice invaded Greece, and especially Xerxes who had set Athens on fire, destroying its temples and, notably, the Acropolis. Diodorus wrote that Alexander threw a huge banquet in the palace of Persepolis for his Companions, during which one of the women present shouted that it would be wonderful if women destroyed what Persians men had spent lifetimes building. Alexander's men shouted back that only Alexander himself would be worthy of leading in the destruction. Mad with drink, Diodorus went on, Alexander, to the music of pipes, flutes and singing, had blazing torches lit and passed around. When they rode away the next day, their heads heavy and their balls emptied, they left 40 still-smoldering columns standing, Persepolis' heritage to this day.

Alexander was wounded far more times than is generally noted. He was wounded by a spear when attacking Gaza, he received an arrow to the leg during another battle and was severely hurt by a stone in still another. He came down with debilitating dysentery, had a lung punctured by an arrow in India, and at one moment, during a revolt of his men, he tried to shame them by claiming that of them all it was he who had received the most wounds, on every part of his body except his back. Arrian gives a very moving description of Alexander's men's reaction to the wound he received in India, that I would like to quote in part: ''Alexander himself also was wounded with an arrow under the breast through his breastplate into the chest, so that Ptolemy says air was breathed in and out of the wound, together with the blood. But although he was faint with exhaustion, he defended himself, as long as his blood was still warm. But with the blood streaming out copiously and without ceasing at every expiration of breath, he was seized with a dizziness and swooning and fell. Peucestas defended him, holding over him the sacred shield brought from Troy.... (Later) Alexander, for fear some attempt at a revolution might be made in the army, had himself conveyed, as soon as it could be done with safety, to the bank of the river Hydraotes. When the ship bearing the king approached the camp, he ordered the tent covering to be removed from the stern, that he might be visible to all. But they were still incredulous, thinking that Alexander's corpse was being conveyed on the vessel until at length he stretched out his hand to the multitude, when the ship was nearing the bank. Then the men raised a cheer, lifting their hands, some towards the sky and others to the king himself. Many even shed involuntary tears at the unexpected sight. Some of the shield-bearing guards brought a litter for him when he was conveyed out of the ship, but he ordered them to fetch his horse. When he was seen again mounting his horse, the whole army re-echoed with loud clapping of hands, so that the banks of the river and the groves near them reverberated with the sound. On approaching his tent he dismounted from his horse, so that he might be seen walking. Then the men came near, some on one side, others on the other, some touching his hands, others his knees, others only his clothes. Some only came close to get a sight of him, and went away having chanted his praise, while others threw garlands upon him, or the flowers which the country of India supplied at that season of the year.''

Arrian lists his personal beauty as his first quality, followed by endurance, intellect, bravery and military genius.

Alexander ordered his Companions to marry Persian women, and Alexander himself had a huge harem--for show, said Cartledge. The men did not prefer the Persian long robes to their light chitons, robes Alexander commanded them to don, nor the effeminate ways of the Orientals, so distant from Macedonian virility. They rejected diadems and other jewelry, proud of the banquets alongside non-perfumed friends and lovers. It was also now that Alexander named Hephaestion Grand Vizier.

A banquet.

Despite the repugnance of the Macedonians to be replaced by the Persians,

Alexander was absolutely determined to weld the two peoples together. As he already dominated Greece, the Western World, he would now, thanks to the assimilation of Persia, be king of the Eastern World as well. Although proof is sketchy, some historians relate that he had sent out feelers to Greece, and especially the Corinthian League founded by his father Philip, concerning his deification. He is reported as having already been deified in Persia, something that may never have crossed the minds of Cyrus, Darius and Xerxes. In addition, Alexander had purportedly also been made pharaoh of Egypt.

Cartledge tells us that for the Greeks in general, and the Macedonians in particular, claiming to be the son of a god, as Alexander did, was acceptable, and was not at all like claiming to be a god, although the Egyptians worshipped him as a living deity.

In 327 he recruited 30,000 Persians. Their *lingua franca* was Aramaic, but the recruits were taught Greek. Alexander made no bones of the fact that these men were to be the core of the new army he would mold, to the Macedonian soldiers' consternation. This, wrote Cartledge, was ''fusion with a vengeance''.

Besides Roxana he took the daughters of Darius III and Artaxerxes III for wives and then, counting on the fertility of Persian women to give him boys, he married off 10,000 Macedonians to oriental wives, giving each a gift. He also obliged 87 of his Companions to do the same in 324. In 334 Alexander sent 2,000 Greek mercenaries to work the mines in Macedonia, the result of which was to inspire the thousands of other Greek mercenaries, who had fought against him, to fight to the death rather than go into ignominious slavery, of which the mines were the very worst example.

Just a word on Roxana. She bore Alexander's son, the future Alexander IV, posthumously. When word came of Alexander's death she had his second wife, Stateira, and his third wife, Parysatis, assassinated. She then put herself under the protection of Alexander's mother, Olympias. Alexander's friends, all former students of Aristotle, united and nominated one of them, Cassander, to take Alexander's place in Macedonia, although for the moment Antipator would act as regent for his son Alexander IV. Antipater had been Philip's second in command and at one time ruled Macedonia for three years while Philip was on campaign. He was so close to Alexander and his mother Olympias that rumor had him Alexander's father. Such was Antipator's preeminence that he was of vital importance in seeing to it that Alexander became king at Philip's death. Although declining the advice of both Antipater and Parmenion to not go to Persia, Alexander left Antipater as regent while in Asia. During Alexander's absence Antipater put down a revolt in Thrace by paying off its king Memnon, the fortuitous result of which were thousands of new recruits for Alexander's army. Antipater also extinguished a revolt by Spartans during which King Agis III was killed. When Alexander heard of the defeat of the Spartans he wrote Antipater, ''It seems that while I've been conquering Darius you've been battling against mice.'' At Alexander's death Antipator battled against those who tried to take his place, finally winning the rule of supreme regent of Alexander's empire. Felled by illness, he left his place to his son Cassander who had Roxana and Alexander IV poisoned, along with a bastard son of Alexander, Heracles, whose mother was the daughter of the Persian satrap Artabazus. With these three dead he turned his attention to Alexander's mother, Olympias, whom he brought to trial, after promising her her freedom should she put herself in his hands peacefully. Instead, she was condemned to death and Cassander turned her over to the relatives of those she had killed--and they were legion. Her body was torn to pieces and she was thrown into the wild without last rites or a tomb, to be devoured by animals. Later Cassander died from the swelling of his members, dropsy, in bed.

Back to Alexander and Hephaestion.

They crossed into India together at the head of hundreds of elephants; together they descended the Indus to the sea. Aristotle had described the two lovers as ''One soul in two bodies.'' This proved to be the case when they both came to Troy, home--thanks to Homer-- of the most famous battle in the history of mankind (3). They laid a wreath on the tomb of Achilles and Patroclus and it was at that moment that Alexander declared that his friendship with Hephaestion was in every point identical to the love between the Trojan lovers. They then ran a race, naked, in honor of the two heroes. Claudius Aelianus, a Roman author and teacher, stated that ''Alexander laid a garland on Achilles' tomb, Hephaestion on Patroclus','' meaning that it was Alexander, the lover, and Hephaestion the belovèd. Yet Alexander and Hephaestion were the same age (Hephaestion a few months older), which certainly implies that they shared all the possibilities of lovemaking without the slightest interest concerning what was customary and what wasn't. Alexander was Hephaestion's king and commander, but would this count in matters sexual? Plutarch tells us that in bed together they would go through Alexander's correspondence. When there was a letter that Alexander wanted kept secret, he would touch his ring to his lover's lips, a wondrously moving example of love, spanning so many centuries, so incredibly numerous life spans, all thanks to Plutarch, certainly as stirred then as the reader now. And, lastly concerning their intimacy, we have the quote from Diogenes of Sinope (see Sources concerning this strange man) who maintained that the only time Alexander was ever vanquished, was by the thighs of Hephaestion.

Alexander

On this coin Alexander is shown sporting the horns of the Egyptian god Ammon. When he visited the Oracle of Siwa he was told, in answer to his question, that he was indeed a god for the simple reason that he had accomplished what no mortal man could.

Another proof of love, some suggest, was Alexander's request that Hephaestion marry his second wife's sister and daughter of Darius. Up until then Hephaestion's name was never mentioned concerning either another man or a woman. Four months after Hephaestion's marriage he was dead, of fever, probably typhus, in Ecbatana. Alexander had been away and didn't arrive back in time to tell his friend goodbye. Plutarch says that his ''grief was uncontrollable''. Alexander had the tails and manes of all the horses shorn and banned music of any sort. One source states that he flung himself on the body and was only dragged away by force, another that ''he lay stretched upon the corpse all day and the whole night.''

As mentioned, the Oracle at Siwa allowed Alexander to have Hephaestion worshipped as a divine hero, but not as a god. Funeral games with 3,000 competitors took place. A pyre 180 feet high, with steps, was raised. It was decorated with ships and banners and figures of armed warriors, torches with snakes entwining them, golden wreaths and eagles, lions and bulls and weapons taken from the enemy. Diodorus recounts that Alexander had the sacred flame in the temple extinguished, an honor exclusively reserved for the deaths of the great Persian kings themselves.

As for Alexander, he died a year later, at age 32, also of fever, also typhus. Some say Aristotle was present. His body was placed in a gold sarcophagus and filled with honey. On its way to Macedonia it was stolen by Ptolemy, an intimate boyhood friend, and taken to Memphis. His successor, Ptolemy II, transferred it to Alexandria where the body was later placed in a sarcophagus made of glass. There it lies today, under unknown sands.

Achilles and Patroclus, Harmodius and Aristogeiton, Epaminondas and Pelopidas, and Alexander and Hephaestion, represent the very best in a couple. All six were united when they were young and beautiful, when their bodies could achieve the utmost in adventure and passion. They all died young too, a terrible sacrifice, indeed, but one that spared them the ravages of demeaning old age. All had one thing in common, wrote Arrian in his *Anabasis*: They strove to better the best.

They also changed the destiny of the world, not only during their time, but for all time.

[Although the above presentation was long, far more information can be gleaned from three of my books: *SPARTA, Alexander and Hephaestion* and *The Sacred Band*.]

Of the principle members of the Order of Chaeronea we know this:

On the gravestone of Montague Summers (1880-1948) one reads an inscription he often repeated in life: ''Tell me strange things.''

And there were few as strange as Summers himself. His ambition was to become an Anglican priest, which he succeeded in doing, and then a Catholic priest when he converted, a title he apparently bestowed on himself, both of which put him in contact with the young boys he delighted in seducing. As this was the ''normal'' routine for priests, then as today, we can leave that very major part of his life and turn to the more original aspects.

He was interested in the occult and in witchcraft, writing *The History of Witchcraft and Demonology*, in which he describes witches as loathsomely obscene, perfectionists in poisoning, blackmail and crime, abortionists who encourage adultery in ladies and lewdness in gentlemen.

He believed in vampires, writing *The Vampire, His Kith and Kin* and *The Vampire in Europe*, and he proclaimed his certainty in the existence of werewolves with his *The Werewolf*. He dressed the part: black soutane, black cloak and black buckled shoes, a man *The Times* called ''A throwback to the Middle Ages.'' He was a member of the British Society for the Study of Sex Psychology, for which he wrote an article on the Marquis de Sade.

John Gambril Nicholson (1866-1931) taught English in a very large number of schools throughout England and Wales, and even coached a football team, manna from Heaven as he liked boys from age 12, one of which he invokes in his autobiographical *Romance of a Choir-Boy*, and a thirteen-year-old, Ernest Mather, to whom he dedicated one of his collections of poems. Poem writing was the *raison d'être* of many homosexuals during the time, with a few, like Byron, making money from their *oeuvre*. He wrote, ''Physical intimacies are but surface emotions, forgotten as soon as they are satisfied; whereas spiritual intimacies live in the heart, they are part of our eternal life, and reach beyond the stars.'' Poppycock he most certainly believed, between bouts of ''physical intimacies''.

Nicholson with Alec Melling, another of his boys, this poor-quality image is the only one available.

Finally, a list of Chaeronea aims, which I adhere to and to which I've added some personal observations between brackets [ ], that the reader can skip over should he wish to do so.

1- To form a social and fraternal secret order for men who love men.

2- To encourage the cultivation of a homosexual, morally, ethically, culturally and spiritually.

3- To use ancient Greece as a model, which includes lover/belovèd consensual, ethical and responsible sexual relations.

4- To aspire to the Greek body ideal [meaning that one must keep oneself in the best possible physical condition, seeking to be as physically erotic as the boy one dreams of sleeping with; this also implies the abandonment of circumcision, which destroys the natural beauty of a boy and lessens a lad's sexual pleasure, especially when self-pleasuring, and no boy is all-boy without his pubic bush].

5- To form an army of lovers to fight against homophobia, to come to the aid of fellow gays, and to contribute to the betterment of one's community.

6- To cease mimicking Judeo-Christian ideals. [Despite incalculable gains in knowledge we still refuse to stand on our own two feet, putting our faith in ourselves rather than superstitious nonsense, fine in times when men had no understanding of disease and death, and needed the encouragement and compassion of an unseen Being bigger than ourselves, beliefs that nonetheless saw, among the Aztecs, perhaps a million hearts of a million lads cut from their young chests and held up, still beating, to the Sun, in hopes it would rise again the following day.]

VICTORIAN SECRETS

In Victorian times a man's sexuality seems to me to have been the strangest that ever existed in our society and was, by its very nature, secret. On the one hand most men seemed to have put women on pedestals and succeeded in controlling their urges, while on the other hand there were never so many male brothels. The sending of telegrams exploded when it was found out that men could hire the boys who delivered them for a few kopeks, a boon for the men, and badly needed additional income for the boys. After all, what a healthy lad did by himself in the privacy of his own room could just as easily be turned into profit, especially as the assignations lasted literally just minutes. Men were often bisexual, and most were encouraged by societal demands to marry. An extraordinarily large number of those like Oscar Wilde--Wilde who craved boys, craved having sex with them and watching, voyeuristically, them having sex together--

married, and there seems to be no doubt that he had no problem in ''honoring'' his wife. Yet boys remained his preference, and he was said to have spent a total of £5,000 on Lord Alfred Douglas, Wilde just one of a string of Victorian sugar daddies.

During the Victorian Era there were far more trials against homosexuals than before 1800 because prudish Victorian police policed what was going on in Victorian bedrooms. The last person executed for homosexuality was in 1835, while the death penalty was dropped only in 1861. Homosexual acts became a misdemeanor in 1885, punishable by 2 years imprisonment. From 1810 to 1835 there were 1,596 prosecutions and 46 executions.

The major symbols of male prostitution were the White Swan Scandal, the Cleveland Street Telegram Scandal and the Oscar Wilde trial. Secret taverns existed from 1700 for male prostitution, and were called molly houses or mollies. Walter's famous *My Secret Life* was published in 1880, in which he paid for sex with a man, ''Yes, Betsy. Get me a nice young cunt without hair on it--and a man to frig.'' And asked her to make sure he was ''no plant, Betsy,'' because the police paid informers (plants) to catch clients.

One of Wilde's interests at the time was Freddie Atkins, 17, that he took to Paris and shared with Maurice Schwabe whom Oscar picked up while there, a threesome Wilde particularly liked because he loved watching two youths having intercourse. Atkins was living with a blackmailer, James Burton, who had Atkins bring johns home and then walk in on them in the middle of sex. The john was blackmailed for criminally assaulting Burton's teenage ''nephew''.

A man can easily have sex daily, which adds up to potentially 300 encounters a year, but Wilde was reported as having as many as four assignations a day. The number of his boys was therefore stupendous, and those that testified during his trials stated that the average price paid was from £2 to £5 (*one 1895 pound--the date of his trial--is worth £130 in 2019*). One of them admitted receiving a silver cigarette case with his name etched in it. There was a lot of fellatio and mutual masturbation, and girls were occasionally invited.

Wilde defended himself by asking why a man shouldn't be allowed to love a boy, rather than a woman, when such was his nature. The problem was that a man of Wilde's intelligence and eloquence could make any boy surrender his ass, not a big deal, perhaps, for streetwise rent boys (10), but if laws hadn't existed to protect the underage one would have found Wilde and other chicken-hawks like him outside of schools.

THE WHITE SWAN SCANDAL
1810

The White Swan was the name given to a house on Vere Street responsible for a major scandal in the 1800s. It was a secret gay club, called a molly house, in which 27 men were arrested, 6 were pilloried and 2 were hung. A total of 200 policemen were employed to protect the arrested men from mob vengeance. The house had upstairs rooms where men of position could meet boys paid to service them. One of the lads was a regimental drummer of 16, Thomas White, one of the hanged. One aristocrat regularly spent a week in the house, going through as many as a dozen boys. Cooks and waiters took part, grenadiers and footmen, as well as a coal-heaver who had two handsome sons the man proudly claimed were as degenerate as he. The boys on the premises could be ''married'' to upper-class sissies in drag, the ceremonies performed before anal intercourse. New recruits, often around age 16, were invited for dinner, put at ease, and initiated in the sex acts they were afterwards paid half a crown to perform. The house was infiltrated by the police that descended on a Sunday, the day chosen for orgies. The men were tried, receiving from 2 to 5 years imprisonment.

The men's ordeal began with their arrests, when mobs formed to scream and pound them with whatever was at hand, from rocks to mud to offal. Although protected by as many as 40 constables at a time, the miscreants were bloodied and whipped by coachmen that the police couldn't hold back.

Six were sentenced to jail and the pillory. The pillories, illustrated below, were located in Haymarket. They could hold four men at a time, the suffering limited to an hour, during which women with baskets of fish guts, rotten eggs, human and animal dung, potatoes, pig blood and dead cats pelted them.

Pillories

When their hour was up they were led away to Newgate Prison—again encrusted with filth, knocked down, kicked and hit with objects on the way, arriving bleeding profusely.

Newgate Prison

The public at times paid with their lives, as the crowds were so dense that embankments gave way, and men and boys fell from trees and rooftops where they'd gone, as numerous as barnacles, to miss nothing of the afflictions.

One of the men who may have played a role in Thomas White's hanging was the Duke of Cumberland whose servant was apparently blackmailing him to hide the Duke's indiscretions with boys and servants like himself. The servant was found with his throat slit, and although the coroner declared he had committed suicide, there was no blood on his hands. One theory is that the duke had visited the White Swan and was White's client. Having the boy hanged was the duke's only hope of escaping scandal, especially as White may have agreed to turn the duke in in exchange for his freedom. White's mother died the day after the boy's murder, of a broken heart, wrote the *Morning Chronicle.*

THE CLEVELAND STREET TELEGRAM SCANDAL
1889

There's an amusing angle to the Cleveland Street Telegram Scandal, in itself a secret organization. Around 1889 there was a sudden increase in the number of telegrams sent between members of the aristocracy and upper classes. It eventually turned out that boys delivering them were highly amenable to exchanging sexual services for a few coins, which in a sense did no one any harm as boys are ever in need of finances to fulfill their desires, while their healthy young bodies can easily care for the sexual wishes of older men, without depleting the lads of their natural ability to ''spend'' (British for ''cum'') nearly at will (with girls, for example, later on during the day or night, should they so wish).

But the boys were found out when the police were called in to investigate the theft of some money in a telegraph office. One of the boys working there, age 15, was searched and a personal fortune was found on him, 14 shillings, equivalent to several weeks' salary. Accused of stealing the sum from the telegraph office, the boy felt it was less damaging to tell the truth, that the money had come from gentlemen who made use of his young person.

Some of the lads.

He gave up the name of the boy, 18, who had recruited him, as well as friends who did the same as he, and added that for additional funds they all worked for a certain Charles Hammond who ran a male brothel on Cleveland Street, frequented, it was rumored, by the man who was next in line for the British throne, Prince Albert Victor, and his squire, Somerset, who fled to Paris before he could be questioned.

The concept that homosexuality was a vice practiced by nobles was reinforced when the Marquess of Queensbury's son was involved with Oscar Wilde.

A cartoon published at the time.

One of the telegraph boys warned Hammond who made an escape, avoiding a possible two-years' imprisonment.

Through his squire Somerset, a lawyer was hired, Arthur Newton, who got the boys off with 4 to 9 months of hard labor. The lawyer got money to Hammond, allowing him to install himself in America. Somerset lived out the rest of his days in the south of France, dying in 1926.

At this time in N.Y., around the Five Points, there were a reported six secret establishments that catered to rent boys and their johns (too secret for additional information).

The boys were young and so the question of the age of consent comes in. The age of consent is when one is permitted to have sexual relations, and has nothing to do with one's majority, which envelops the age of criminal responsibility, voting, driving and drinking.

In Ancient Greece a boy married around age 30, leaving him lots of time to play the field (although marriage did little to block him afterwards), whereas in Rome Augustus wanted his citizens to have children before age 30, and heavily fined them if they didn't, because the state was in dire need of men for wars, the running of government, for agriculture, construction, etc. Girls married around puberty or a little afterwards.

In Medieval Europe one could marry between ages 12 to 14, and in the 1500s and 1600s girls could have intercourse around age 12. After the French revolution, which abolished laws against homosexuality, intercourse was allowed at age 11, and Spain, Portugal and Denmark followed with the age of consent between ages 10 and 12.

In the 1800s the age increased to around age 13, while in the 1900s it was raised to 16 as one became aware of sexual abuse concerning girls. It went to between ages 16 and 18 in the U.S. in 1920 thanks to female reformers. Only Spain held out, allowing intercourse at age 12, and that to 1999 (!), when it increased to age 13 (!), and only in 2015 did it go to age 16, but as we all know, everything ripens faster in sunny Spain.

To my way of thinking, 16 would be perfect (although kids in the Internet Age frequently replace masturbation by intercourse around age 15).

Canada, where the age of consent is 16, allows sex between ages 14 and 15 if the partner is not more than 5 years older, and between ages 12 to 13 if the partner is less than 2 years older. The age of consent in Finland is 16, but anyone can have sex at any age if they're the same age.

Kids must nonetheless be protected from *adults* who have the power of experience, wealth and position, in which case no law can be harsh enough. (Tut-tut.)

SKULL AND BONES
1832

The Skull and Bones is a Yale University extremely-secret society founded in 1832. ''The mystery attending its existence forms the one great enigma which college gossip never tires of discussing,'' wrote Lyman Bagg in his book *Four Years at Yale*, 1871. In addition to the society's principle building, called the Tomb, they have a retreat on Deer Island in the St. Lawrence River, the meals catered to by stewards. Basically male, rich, well-connected and Protestant, women were permitted entrance in 1992. Members are awarded nicknames, ''Long Devil'' supposedly given to the tallest, Henry Luce was ''Baal'', ''magogs'' are the most sexually experienced, ''gogs'' the least.

The Tomb and Deer Island retreat.

During their initiation (at least in former times) the boys were said to have been beaten before lying in a coffin and detailing their sexual lives while masturbating, the whole representing ''rebirth''. The society's secrecy has held out for nearly two hundred years, an achievement in our age, proof of the solidity of the friendships formed during the boys' Yale years and afterwards. That said, members are so highly placed in American government that they would gain nothing from disclosure, and at any rate what went on was probably childish nonsense in comparison to their later responsibilities, which included two presidents who had a finger inches away from the button that could activate nuclear annihilation.

Homosexuality is suspected and often referred to--as in any grouping of males--but there is no proof that there was or is any more homosexual hoopla than in the population at large.

THE APOSTLES
1820
Maynard Keynes – Kim Philby – Guy Burgess – Anthony Blunt – Alfred Tennyson – William Cory – Oscar Browning – G.E. Moore – J.A. Symonds – Ludwig Wittgenstein – Bertrand Russell – Rupert Brooke

The Apostles is a Cambridge University discussion group founded in 1820, originally 12 in number, from which came the name. Meetings are held Saturday evenings, refreshments consisting of coffee and Whales, sardines on toast. Undergraduate members, the most numerous, are called embryos, former members angels. The group's papers are kept in a cedar chest they've dubbed the Ark. Eleven of the original 12 were buried in the same cemetery, proof of the group's cohesion until death.

Some of the subjects of debate were ''Is self abuse bad as an end?'' (most voting No!) and one debate was entitled, ''Achilles or Patroclus,'' supposedly meaning lust against friendship.

Most of the members of the Apostles were also part of the Bloomsbury Set, related in detail in the following chapter. Rupert Brooke was an Apostle but outside the Set, the reason why his biography will immediately follow, along with more details on Maynard Keynes and Brooke's dedicated friend Denis Browne.

Homosexual traitors Kim Philby, Guy Burgess, Donald Maclean and Anthony Blunt were also Apostle members, among other Apostle traitors, most of whom were homosexuals. Maynard Keynes was a man whose obsession with numbers led to his noting his blowjobs, his wanking and his passive pursuit of sodomy. He loved Mediterranean islands where lads were cheap and boy whorehouses common. The license to fuck children was part of an Englishman's aristocratic rights, the basis being English Boarding Schools where they themselves were plugged even before reaching puberty (see my book *Boarding School Homosexuality*).

Richard Deacon in his excellent *The Cambridge Apostles*, 1985, wrote this about Blunt: ''He was so fastidious, so aesthetic, so unpuritanically witty and charming that he never seemed to be what he was.'' And concerning Burgess: He was a charmer who had friends in all walks of life, ''a supremely brilliant talker and in many ways an original and serious historian.''

Victor Rothschild was an Apostle who suggested the entry of Blunt into the Apostles and rented a house to Burgess. He supposedly gave away nuclear secrets to Israel, Israel who gained the atomic bomb thanks to French president Charles de Gaulle who first saved France during W.W. II, and then Israel to whom he disclosed how to fabricate the bomb, thanks to which no one now dares attack it. Otherwise Rothschild is reported to have said that there was no place in Britain for poor Jews, and only rich and influential Jews should be allowed entry into Israel itself.

One of the first embryos, Frederick Maurice, encouraged members to give up their inner thoughts, confessions that were analyzed and debated, the antithesis of what went on during the times when free thought was stifled because it was considered embarrassing and too personal for one to disclose intimate aspects of one's life. Soul-searching introspection was eased by drugs such as opium, and members were encouraged to experiment in this and other domains. (Freud himself encouraged the use of cocaine at the time of its invention [2].)

Two Apostles who did not hide their homosexuality were Alfred Tennyson and Arthur Hallam, homosexuality which, added to Apostle interest in psychology, experimentation in drugs and other liberalities, became the founding cement that ultimately was responsible for the Apostles' success in gaining a larger membership as well as becoming increasingly secret in order to cover up Society ''research''. As Richard Deacon writes, love between members was ''the beginning of a kind of sublimated homosexual cult within the Society.'' Of the Tennyson/Hallam couple another member, Frances Brookfield, declared ''our minds are dazzled by the Apostles' achievements, and our hearts are warmed by their mutual love.''

Hallam died only four years after being elected an Apostle and Tennyson wrote,
''Forgive my grief for one removed,
The creature whom I found so fair.''

Tennyson and the fair Hallam. Called *le jeune homme fatal* thanks to his beauty, Hallam (1811-1833) went from Eton to Trinity College Cambridge and into the Apostles where as an 18-year-old he slept with Tennyson, 20, and proposed marriage to Tennyson's sister, par for the course in those times as described in the chapter on the Bloomsbury Set. On holiday in Vienna he caught a chill and the resulting fever carried him off in his sleep at age 22.

Apostle boys were "eager to savour new experiences and explore new horizons,'" wrote Deacon. John Sterling wrote, "Commend me to the brethren, who, I trust, are waxing daily in religion and radicalism.... To my education in that Society I feel I owe every power I possess.... From the Apostles I, at least, learned to think as a free man."

The discovery of sex that went on in all boarding schools was just that: the occasion for boys to explore their bodies and the immense pleasure they could offer each other. Some went on to become heterosexual, some homosexual, most omnisexual (13), but in all cases the mystic discovery of first love would remain an integral part of them until death. Most of the boys fathered sons of their own, boys for whom they had great sexual tolerance thanks to the countless nights when the men themselves had experienced first bliss, first love and first pain, beside, and often inside, one of their own.

Those with especially developed homosexual affinities found a welcome compost in the Apostles, and as Apostle members opened their ranks to boys known for their homosexual preferences, the ranks of those who practiced what they called Socratic love (4) exponentially enlarged. Like today's gays who flock to Hollywood, San Francisco and Miami thanks to the affable climate--avoiding positions like judges and politicians where discovery would see them eliminated by popular vote--so too did word get out that the Apostles was the place to be for boys who did boys. The emotional experiences of boyish exploration continued as love between youths and, finally, the love of men for boys, as Apostles who had been students became school masters, predators of lads just immerging from puberty.

William Johnson Cory, for example, an Apostle who was characterized as ''the most brilliant Eton tutor of his day,'' loved by his students who called him Tute (for tutor), ''the wisest master who has ever been to Eton,'' stated a colleague. He wrote a justification for learning Latin, stating that it ''enforced the habit of attention ... assuming at a moment's notice a new intellectual position ... entering quickly into another's intellectual thoughts ... (encouraging) minute points of accuracy ... and mental soberness.''

He penned a book of poems, *Ionica*, dedicated to pretty-faced Charles Wood, that laid ''down the principle that affection between people of the same sex is no less natural and irrational than the ordinary passionate relations.''

After 27 years at Eton he was forced to retire due to improper conduct with boys, of whom Eton was a limitless source.

Oscar Browning was partially known for his feud with Virginia Woolf who accused him of not only thinking that ''the best woman was intellectually inferior to the worst man,'' but she outed his preference for boys.

Browning was educated at Eton, a student of William Johnson Cory. He went on to King's College, Cambridge, where he became a fellow and a member of the Apostles.

He was dismissed from Eton as a result of a homosexual scandal there, in 1875. He went on to teach at Cambridge and founded a training college for teachers. He was also president of the Cambridge Footlights. His nephew and biographer purportedly destroyed his diaries and letters as protection against further scandal concerning his involvement with young men. (Only thanks to diaries that have survived do we know a little about the sex lives of Roger Casement, Keynes and a few others.)

In love with Italy like so many before him, Browning died in Rome in 1923.

Boys who went to Cambridge were the chosen few, those who had inherited the earth, and they knew it. Charles Merivale, later Dean of Ely, was an Apostle who stated that Apostles were comfortable among themselves because they had common intellectual tastes and aspirations, mutually flattering each other, mutually conceited, and that it was up to them to enlighten the rest of the world: "We lived in constant intercourse with one another, day by day, met over our wine and our tobacco." To this Richard Deacon adds: "It was in such intercourse in the rooms of individual members of the Society that homosexuality flourished."

As I wrote in my book *Boarding School Homosexuality*, most of these lads went on to marry, as did Wilde, but the marriages were rarely sexually fulfilling, as the heat and lust of first love can never be excelled.

The underlying fact that men faced prison for their acts only reinforced the luck they had to find themselves in the protected walls of the Apostles, where imprisonment *à la* Oscar Wilde was an impossibility. Godsworthy Lowes Dickinson, an Apostle, suggested also that homosexuals escaped public wrath because people, like the Queensberrys, did not suspect that sex was going on just because two men lived together.

It was Goldsworthy who initiated the idea of the League of Nations. Called Goldie, he was in love with Roger Frey that we meet in the Bloomsbury Set, perhaps platonically as Fry was heterosexual and Dickinson's philosophy was based on Neo-Platonism (although nearly all claimed virginal Platonism, before and after joint orgasms).

Goldie entered the boarding school of Beomonds, then Charterhouse School, from ages 14 to 19, followed by King's College, Cambridge. In 1896 he wrote *The Greek View of Life*. E.M. Forster wrote the biography of Dickinson after Dickinson's death in 1932 but omitted all information concerning Dickinson's homosexuality and foot fetishism. Dickinson wrote dozens of books, one of which was *The Magic Flute: A Fantasia to Plato and his Dialogues*. His relationships with young men were both sexual and fatherly, certainly an ideal figure for a boy needing warm guidance from a man who would show him the way, instructing him intellectually while satisfying him tenderly and physically, yet lacking the virile dimension so vital in Ancient Greece (for the simple reason that most dons were swishy pansies).

Dickinson was reputed as having been remarkably candid in exposing Platonic homoerotism by stating, ''That there was another side to the matter goes without saying. This passion, like any other, has its depths, as well as its heights.'' Daring for the times, apparently. Paul Robinson summarized Dickinson's sexual life as ''an intensely romantic attachment, passionate kisses and warm embraces (with a hint of fetishism [feet]), followed by relief by masturbation.'' Dickinson himself confessed to masturbating, when young, over his father's boots.

The expression Higher Sodomy was now invented. In the chapter on the Bloomsbury Set I define it as meaning a Platonic approach to homosexuality, while in the Apostles it apparently also meant Higher in the sense that love between men was infinitely more valorizing than that between men and women. In fact, there was nothing Platonic about their relations: these men were fucking each other.

Julian Bell was an Apostle whose parents and their Feydeauesque lives is covered in the Bloomsbury Set. Bell (1908-1937) was the love interest of both Blunt and Burgess, but it's not clear who got the boy, although *both* is the probable answer. A poet, he taught English in China and was killed in the Spanish Civil war at age 29.

Homosexuality has always survived, despite the lead blanket of Christianity, and for many Apostles homosexuality was a way of showing one's revolt over church beliefs. And then, one could find solace even for those who continued to believe, as James I pointed out when he said, before his Council, ''I, James, am neither a god nor an angel, but a man like any other. Therefore I act like a man, and confess to loving those dear to me more than other men. You may be sure that I love the Duke of Buckingham more than anyone else. I wish to speak in my own behalf and not to have it thought to be a defect, for Jesus Christ did the same and therefore I cannot be blamed. Christ had his John, and I have my George.''

The philosopher G.E. Moore's sexuality is hard to discern, although philosophically he went from a passionate believer in God to a man who gave up his faith, stating that one ''should spread skepticism until at last everyone knows we can know absolutely nothing." Homosexuality became a "must" in the Society, to the extent that Duncan Grant of the Bloomsbury Set went on to say that "even the womanizers pretend to be sods, lest they shouldn't be thought respectable."

Frederic William Henry Myers (1843-1901) was a devoted--meaning highly randy--Apostle homosexual, two of whose bed companions were J.A. Symonds and Henry Sidgwick. Later in life he was said to have been as enthusiastically heterosexual as homosexual (one of his maidens committed suicide in the tradition of Virginia Woolf). He seems to have replaced religion with psychical research, spending the rest of his life with mediums, spiritualists, the paranormal and telepathy, and was said to have swallowed any charlatan tomfoolery that came his way. He also used his psychical research as a means of fulfilling his need for voyeuristic sex, thanks to his deep delving into the intimate aspects of his subjects' lives.

Henry Sidgwick, philosopher and economist (1838-1900), founded the Society of Psychical Research with his lover Myers and others. An agnostic--as were many Apostles at some time in their lives, although an amazing number seem to have converted to

Catholicism near the end--he had difficulty coming to terms with his homosexuality, as did Symonds, which may in part have led to his marrying. If I might take a bit of a detour: Richard Deacon brings us a quote from Piers Paul Read who had spoken with some Apostles. Read wrote that when ''I mentioned Plato, Kant, Nietzsche, Marx or Sartre, I was treated with a pained smile, or a scoffing laugh ... such speculative, continental fun-philosophies were considered quite outside the bounds of serious study.'' The Apostles obviously considered themselves brilliant, yet their bumbling approach to sexuality--from the extreme of publicly humping each other in dormitories to the lows of submitting to highly unfulfilling marriages--leaves me perplex at their inability to confront something as mundane as sex, and this despite their belief in their own stellar genius. Added to this was the silliness of the séances men like Sidgwick attended, as far afield as Paris and Naples.

Sidgwick

Roden Noel (1834-1894) was enamored of his own body: ''I was immensely vain of my physical beauty,'' and claimed that the homosexual part of his bisexuality was inherited from his great uncle, Percy Jocelyn, forced to flee London when found in the arms of a soldier. His first sexual memory as a little boy was being caressed by his father's footman. He was also said to have been the first to have fucked Symonds. Selected extracts from his works include: ''eyes dim-dewy with desire, appleblooming boys, bronze harvestmen, his back so tender.'' As with Proust who disguised his boys as women in order for his *oeuvre* to be published, one can only wonder at what marvels men like Noel,

Byron, and others could have come up with had laws and society allowed freedom of artistic expression.

Noel by George Richmond.

Lytton Strachey, covered in the chapter on the Bloomsbury Set, was responsible for the Ark, the trunk in which the Apostles kept their secret papers, and used its private content to unmask Apostle homosexual members, which aided his search for young prey. Strachey, good-looking as a very young boy, compensated for later homeliness by developing a cunning, Machiavelli presence that, combined with manipulative genius, brought him to the center of Apostle power, a man one had to content sexually if one wished entry into the Society, a dictator whose impact influenced countless books written at the time. Strachey worked in tandem with Maynard

Keynes, both who raised the love of boys to a veritable godly level (didn't Zeus have his Ganymede and Apollo his Hyacinth [5], as well as James I his George?). When Keynes went on to marry, the shock of his treason equaled that of Burgess's, stated one Apostle. Both Keynes and Strachey vetted new embryos, and beauty replaced the criteria of brains, although an aristocratic background continued to have importance, albeit well behind sexual promise. Arthur Hobhouse, for example (see the Bloomsbury Set) was chosen and immediately seduced by Keynes, Keynes who signed his letters to Hobhouse ''Your constant true love, JMK''.

Hobhouse

The appeal of the Society must have been an enormous magnet for boys looking for other handsome boys, thanks to Strachey and Keynes's selections, and the Apostles became ever-more secret because, as Strachey wrote Keynes, people in general, and ''dowagers'' in particular, would never accept the image of boys inserting their dicks in the asses of other boys, my choice of words for Strachey's more refined comment that ''the best among the Apostles were sodomitical.''

A change apparently took place, after the Strachey/Keynes tandem, with the election of the homosexual Ludwig Wittgenstein who wanted the Apostles known for other things than a homosexual harem, especially when he had to keep his own favorites from the roving hands of Apostle members.

Ludwig Wittgenstein

Bertrand Russell taught Wittgenstein at Cambridge (1889-1955) and found him "the most perfect example I have ever known of genius as traditionally conceived; passionate, profound, intense." Born in Vienna into a *richissime* family (Brahms and Mahler regularly gave concerts in their homes), their extreme wealth did not keep three of his brothers from committing suicide. His *Philosophical Investigations*, studies in the philosophy of mathematics, of the mind and of language, was published after his death. The family, formerly Jews, were baptized Catholics and Wittgenstein was deeply devoted to Christianity before becoming agnostic. All the brothers, five, were intellectual in the extreme. Wittgenstein never forgot his Jewish heritage and blamed it for his imperfection, saying that "even the greatest Jewish thinker is no more than talented, myself for instance." He was in the same school and class as Hitler, but then Hitler was held back a grade and Wittgenstein advanced a grade, so they may not have met. Had Russell been homosexual he would have taken Wittgenstein as a lover, stating, "I love him. He is *the* young man one hopes for."

Wittgenstein's three known lovers were David Pinsent, Francis Skinner and Ben Richards.

Pinset and Wittgenstein; Richards and Wittgenstein.

Wittgenstein joined the Austro-Hungarian Army in W.W.I fighting the British. His repeated bravery won him innumerable medals. Physically and mentally spent after the war, he became an elementary and then a primary school teacher and a monastery gardener, a multi-millionaire who lived in one room with bed and washstand, his meals consisting, according to a visitor, of coarse bread, butter and cocoa. Back at Cambridge Wittgenstein wrote his thesis for a PhD that philosophers Russell and Moore were given to read, Wittgenstein telling them, ''Don't worry. I know you'll never

understand it.'' Wittgenstein wasn't arrogant so much as he simply believed in his absolute superiority. When he went to Cambridge Keynes remarked, ''Well, God has arrived. I met him on the 5.15 train.'' In fact, Wittgenstein took over Moore's chair in philosophy, after which he became a British citizen. When his former lover Francis Skinner died in 1941 Wittgenstein took up with Skinner's teenage friend Keith Kirk. He died simply stating ''I've had a wonderful life.'' [The *Wikipedia* article on Wittgenstein is of extraordinary brilliance.]

Deacon points out that whereas being called ''my dear boy'' in Strachey/Keynes times was a coveted compliment, after Wittgenstein it became a slap in the face, illustrated by an Apostle angel, Sir John Sheppard, who referred to a fellow Apostle as ''my very own precious boy,'' getting, in response, this admonition: ''I am not a boy, I am not precious and I am in no way whatsoever yours or anyone else's boy.'' Unheard of until then.

Sexual exploits in the Apostles became more muted, although Deacon does refer to an Apostle dinner that took place later, in 1937, after which the boys retired to the home of Eddie Marsh for an all-night orgy. This reveals a great deal about what had been going on throughout the years, but Deacon mentioned it as a bacchanalia that marked the end of an era, meaning that sexual hijinks went on, but more muzzled. (Let us not forget the royal recently filmed with his pants down during a Vegas heterosexual orgy with, apparently, prostitutes, proof that boys will never ever cease being boys. The only unsavory aspect is that these people the Brits call royals continue, through the mere accident of birth, to lord it over a people who drool at their feet).

Marsh standing behind Winston Churchill,

1907.
Marsh was Churchill's private secretary for
21 years, and was knighted upon retirement.
He was an influent Apostle and collected
works of art produced by the Bloomsbury Set,
with whom he was intimately involved.

Rupert Brooke
1887 – 1915
Maynard Keynes – Denis Browne

Rupert Brooke is often cited for the letter he wrote concerning his plan to seduce a young friend. The letter is cold and calculating, and once he did get the lad's shorts down, one cares little for the lack of passion that followed. This was supposedly Brooke's first attempt at losing his burdensome virginity, homosexually speaking, as he had apparently ''known'' girls for some time. He was so startlingly good-looking that he was certainly prey from his earliest years, and because sex is what took place in boarding schools, days and especially nights, and given the nature of adolescent lust, and the fact that lads at the time took their sex very seriously, the boy he said he'd seduced in his letter was certainly far from the first.

Rupert Brooke

The problem evaluating Brooke's work is that one can't see the forest for the trees, the trees here being his beauty. He was president of the Cambridge Fabian Society and a founder of the Marlowe Society, a drama club in which he acted in its plays. How many students were members thanks to their literary appeal and how many were there-- boys and girls--drawn by Brooke's beauty can't be known. Born in Rugby, in 1887, he is reputed for his First World War poetry, appeals for young men to engage in the services and commit mass suicide, his most celebrated poem being this:

If I should die, think only this of me:

That there's some corner of a foreign field
That is forever England. There shall be
In that rich earth a richer dust concealed;
A dust whom England bore, shaped, made
aware,
Gave, once, her flowers to love, her ways to
roam,
A body of England's, breathing English air,
Washed by the rivers, blest by suns of home.

He was bisexual, having perhaps fathered a daughter on a visit to Tahiti. He was an Apostle and part of the Bloomsbury Set, with homosexuals E.M. Forster and John Maynard Keynes, a genius on economics who is daily cited somewhere in this world to our own day. Keynes's father was a professor of economics at Cambridge. Keynes's life was one brilliant exploit after another, during his college days and afterwards, in economics although his chief interest was philosophy. He represented the British Treasury at Versailles in 1918 and when he couldn't protect the German people from financial catastrophe, he resigned. Keynes was open about his homosexuality. His diaries were heavily encoded but he had an obsession with numbers since childhood and noted everything. He wrote having sex with ''a 16-year-old under Etna'' and ''the liftboy of Vauxhall''. In 1911, as one example, he had 16 C's, 4 A's and 5 W's. Enciphers guess that the A's were ass-contacts, the C's cocksucking and the W's wanks (jerking off) with boys/men. He married a ballerina in Diaghilev's Ballets Russes in 1925, a marriage that lasted 20 years. He died of a heart attack in 1946.

Rupert Brook

Brooke had numerous lovers and friends, one of whom caught the ear of Winston Churchill who commissioned Brooke into the Royal Naval Volunteer Reserve, an honor Brooke accepted on the condition that his friend Denis Browne, a composer, be commissioned too. It was in Denis's arms on the island of Skyros that Brooke … well, let Denis tell it: "At 4 o'clock he became weaker, and at 4:46 he died, with the sun shining all round his cabin, and the cool sea-breeze blowing through the door and the shaded windows. No one could have wished for a quieter or a calmer end than in that lovely boy, shielded by the mountains and fragrant with sage and thyme." No one was luckier too to have a friend like Denis Browne.

Brooke died from a simple mosquito bite that had become infected. Denis died in battle at Gallipoli. His last letter was found in his wallet, that he'd put there knowing he hadn't long to live: "I'm luckier than Rupert because I've fought. But there's no one to bury me as I buried him, so perhaps he's best off in the long run."

Facing a Nazi firing squad Willem Arondeus had cried out: "Let it be known that homosexuals are not cowards!" Such was the case of Denis Browne.

THE BLOOMSBURY SET
1912 – 1941
Duncan Grant – Vanessa Bell – Virginia Wolfe – Maynard Keynes – Arthur Hobhouse – Paul Roche – A.L. Rowse – G.E. Moore –

Roger Fry – Aldous Huxley – E.M. Forest – Lytton Strachey – Mark Gertler

To understand the Bloomsbury Set one must understand the French expression *panier de crabes*, a basket of crabs, crawling over and through each other, fucking, yes, but also biting, their claws fully deployed.

A perfect example of this was Duncan Grant's relationship with Vanessa Bell. Duncan, a painter and a homosexual who had had exclusively homosexual encounters in boarding schools since puberty, decided to live with Vanessa who was nonetheless married but whose husband was off elsewhere with mistresses. Vanessa (the sister of Virginia Wolfe) badly wanted a child from the supremely handsome Duncan who agreed to move in with her for the time needed to get her pregnant, and immediately afterwards sexual relations ceased between the two while awaiting the birth of their little girl, Angelica, who was given Bell's name, Bell who pretended to be her father.

Duncan Grant

Duncan stayed on with Vanessa, which in no way inhibited his taking numerous lovers, for 40 years, until her death. One of his lovers was David Garnett who later married Angelica. Garnett was thusly fucking the father *and* the father's daughter! (although, presumably, not at the same time).

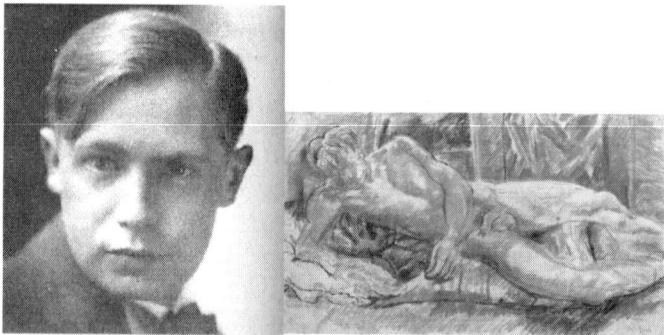

David Garnett by Duncan.

Maynard Keynes said Duncan Grant had been the love of his life. From his youth Duncan had been one of Lytton Strachey's lovers, Strachey who was also his cousin. He was also the lover of Arthur Hobhouse. Hobhouse entered Eton at age 11 and then Balliol College, Oxford, seven years later. He had his own law practice, was on the board of a charity commission, worked as a law member for the council of the Governor-General of India, and was on the Judicial Committee of the Privy Council when he returned from India to London. He received a peerage as Baron Hobhouse, married and died without children.

Duncan Grant with Keynes, the love of Keynes's life.

Duncan was kept during his later life by Paul Roche and it was on Roche's estate that he died.

Roche by Duncan Grant.

Duncan was born in 1885, just six months before the passing of the Criminal Law Act that criminalized male homosexual acts in England, regardless of consent, an act used to convict Oscar Wilde in 1895. It was also dubbed the blackmailer's act because it was profitably used by hundreds of blackmailers afterwards. The fear of discovery was such that even later writers on Greek love, such as A.L. Rowse and Kenneth Dover, claimed to have been happily married, which, conceivably, could have been true.

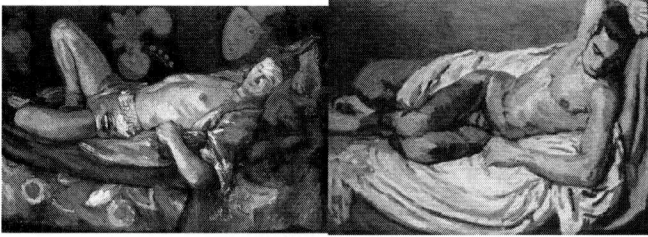

Paul Roche by Duncan.

Duncan went to prep schools in Rugby and London before entering the Westminster School of Art at age 17.

Hyllus by Duncan.

What seems incredible, at least to me, is that men like Grant were having sex with some of the homeliest men living then. Of course I'll be accused of being shallow, but a man does have to get hard to have good sex, and how can one do so in the presence of men like Keynes and Garnett?

Paul Roche and perhaps an example of boarding-school fun, by Duncan Grant.

Paintings by Duncan are innumerable, and I've included a number here for the pleasure of the senses.

Leigh Farnell, one of Duncan's very first boarding-school friends,

with whom he remained close all his life.

Duncan was unanimously described as being a good person and those who cared for him at the end of his life found him ''impishly benign'', with great personal charm. He admired the philosopher G. E. Moore and told the boys who gave access to his old hands that he owed all of his moral philosophy to Moore, ''which possibly does not amount to much,'' said Moore.

Duncan Grant of himself.

Another of his daughter's lovers, who had also been *his* lover, was George Bergen:

George Bergen

David Garnett, Grant's lover and Angelica's husband, was called Bunny since his childhood due to a rabbit cloak given to him then. When he married Angelica her parents were said to have been scandalized (although *which* parents, Vanessa and Bell or Vanessa and Grant, is not known). Garnett was an author, founded the Nonesuch Press and ran a bookshop. From a first wife he had had two sons and with Angelica four daughters before they separated. He died in France in 1981 at age 89.

Paul Roche was a novelist, poet and Greek and Latin translator, and was associated with the Bloomsbury Set. He was an ordained priest and married twice, fathering five children. Although Roche's last wife was against his taking in his lover, Duncan was imposed on the household but was said to have cooled things down out of respect for Roche's wife although, of course, men always succeed in getting what they want, in one secret place or another, so the cooling was most probably due to a greater desire to have sex with others than themselves.

Grant and David Garnett.

Duncan Grant died in 1978 at age 93 and Roche at age 91 in 2007. They had been together 32 years.

Paul Roche

Roche and Duncan's love had been the closest, the deepest, the truest of friendships, and Roche closed the chapter on their lives in this way: ''I could see that he was in a very bad way, breathing heavily.... Dr Cooper said to me, 'I can't save him this time, he's too far gone, and it's much better to let him go'. So I agreed to that. Duncan lay on the bed.... I came up to him the night before he died... This is what I think I said, or the gist of it.... 'Duncan, you have nothing to worry about, whatever you have done in life that you are sorry for, God loves you, whatever you've done, He loves you. You don't have to worry about anything. You're in His hands, and so you can sleep peacefully and everything is ok.... Don't think that God is angry with anything.... He's not, He loves you.' Duncan was incapable of speaking ... so I quietly left the room.... When I came back in the morning ... I realised Duncan was dead. That was an enormous shock to me.... I went to Firle to be at the funeral, but I suddenly found that I couldn't stand, every time I stood up I simply collapsed onto the floor.''

Duncan Grant's *The Bathers*.

One of the characteristics of the Bloomsbury Set, besides the fact that most lived so long, was that many ended up spending the last of their lives with women, as did Lytton Strachey and Maynard Keynes.

The Set was against what Roger Fry (who was an Apostle and who had been Vanessa Bell's lover) called Post-Impressionists, although Fry, an artist and art critic, defended it. Loved by many Bloomsbury members, male and female, he seems to have been heterosexual. His list of Post-Impressionists includes Cézanne, Gauguin, van Gogh and Seurat, to which he later added Rousseau and Toulouse-Lautrec. Many of the Set thought the Post-Impressionists were trivial in their art, reducing objects to basic shapes, while Seurat even painted tiny dots that some called Scientific-Impressionism. Van Gogh used lavish brush strokes to convey his feelings and states of mind, and Cézanne tried to bring purity in his art by reducing objects to basic shapes.

Roger Fry

Lytton Strachey, one of the founders of the Bloomsbury Set, seduced them all, and although he was presentable when very young,

I have no idea how he did it later on, especially when he grew the beard he was so proud of, but that most others found ridiculous.

One of 13 children, Lytton is the 3rd from the left.

Perhaps Roy Campbell, a poet and satirist, had him in mind when he said that the Set was a group of ''sexless folk whose sexes intersect.'' Some, happily, were far from being sexless. Duncan Grant was gorgeous, and when Strachey had intercourse with him he said that he felt joy because Grant was so moved and that what he loved ''more than the consummation of my own poor pleasure … was that for the first time I loved his soul,'' a need by the Set to introduce Plato somewhere in their sexual musical chairs. As a lad Strachey justified sex by saying that ''I may be sinning, but I am doing it in the company of Greece" in reference to Socrates and other texts on Hellenic love. Strachey goes on and on about the ideal love, the meeting of the minds, but Roger Senhouse, a student of Eton and Oxford University and owner of the publishing house that published Colette, Orwell and Günter Grass, said his relationship with Strachey had been sadomasochistic. In the same way that Plato went on about Platonic love, stating that "evil is the vulgar lover who loves the body rather than the soul," Plato and Socrates had nonetheless special permission to attend the athletic preparation of boys, where adults were banned by law, to enjoy the beauty of youthful dicks with their first pubic down, and hairless asses.

Strachey: He was proud of the reddish hue of his beard.

Strachey wrote his book *Ermyntrude and Esmeralda* in 1913, published in 1969, long after his death, in which two innocent girls titter about the ''absurd little things that men have in statues between their legs.'' When the girls asked a priest what love is, he replies ''the sanctification of something'', unless the object is a member of the same sex. A father banishes his son for having sex with his tutor, but the son claims that he was only doing what the Athenians did and, anyway, his father ''had done the same when he was a boy in school but had forgotten about it.''

Strachey's school was Trinity College, Cambridge, where he had sexual relations with Clive Bell who married Vanessa who would have sexual relations with Duncan Grant who would have sexual relations with Strachey and David Garnett, Garnett who would have sexual relations with Duncan Grant and, later, Grant's daughter Angelica, as reported. Bloomsbury was a location in central London encompassing Gordon and Fitzroy Squares. The aim of Bloomsbury was ''to get a maximum of pleasure out of their personal relations. If this meant triangles or more complicated geographical figures, well then, one accepted that too.''

Strachey's hallmark was biography, combining psychology with sympathy for the subject, irreverence and wit. He wrote *Queen Victoria, Eminent Victorians* and *Elizabeth and Essex.* An example of his wit: He described Florence Nightingale as employing soldiers' wives to clean her laundry. When Strachey, a pacifist, was asked what he would do if a Hun tried to rape his sister, he answered: ''I would insert my body between them.'' While others seduced by making girls laugh, he did so through spell-binding eloquence (maintained his admirers).

In another of those strange Bloomsbury multi-cornered sexual relationships, Strachey lived with Dora Carrington who adored him and she married *his* lover Ralph Partridge, not for love, but to bring Strachey closer to her. At the same time he was seeing other men, one of whom was Roger Senhouse, with whom he had his sadomasochistic arrangement, one that went so far as to include mock crucifixions. Strachey paid for the marriage between Carrington and Partridge and, naturally, accompanied them on their honeymoon to Venice. Carrington had a boy's haircut and appreciated girls, while her new husband was said to have genuinely loved her. Strachey bought the newlyweds a house. Partridge left her for another woman and she became pregnant by another man who asked her to leave Strachey. She chose instead to abort. Around this time Aldous Huxley fell in love with her, ''Her short hair, clipped like a page's.... She had large blue china eyes ... of puzzled earnestness.''

Carrington and Strachey, Huxley and Senhouse.

The plot thickens: Ralph Partridge had left both Carrington and Strachey for another woman, Frances Marshall, who took up with Ralph because she knew he was Strachey's lover, and as she *also* loved Strachey she thought her proximity with Ralph would bring her closer to Strachey.

Strachey and Partridge.

When Strachey died in 1932 at age 51 from stomach cancer, Carrington committed suicide.

Strachey must have been a force of nature because he was a character in nearly all the books his friends wrote before and after his death.

The intrigue doesn't end here: The painter Mark Gertler adored Carrington to the point of obsession. Incapable of understanding why she preferred a homosexual to him, he bought a revolver and threatened to kill himself when she married Strachey's lover Ralph Partridge. Gertler did finally commit suicide in 1939 at age 48. Today his paintings are worth millions.

Mark Gertler, said to have been a beauty.

In her diary Virginia Woolf wrote that she was glad to be alive and couldn't imagine why Carrington had killed herself. Ten years later, in 1941, Virginia did the same, by drowning.

E.M. Forster was above all a humanist, acknowledged as such when named President of Cambridge Humanists in 1959 and a member of the British Humanist Association from 1963 until his death in 1970 at age 81. A great aunt left him £800,000 in today's money, which freed him from any form of servitude. He was an Apostle who was an on-the-fringe member of Bloomsbury, and a Kings College, Cambridge, student. His name is associated with several men, among them Isherwood and Benjamin Britten.

His travels took him throughout Europe, especially Italy, which inspired two books, *Where Angels Fear to Tread* and *A Room with a View*. He was secretary to a maharaja and several visits to India inspired his most read book, *A Passage to India*.

Among what is called his ''loving relationships'' was a very long one with a married policeman.

He was nominated for the Nobel Prize 13 times! He wrote his last book at age 35.

EARLY AMERICA
Henry Gerber, John Adams, Magnus Hirschfeld, Von Steuben

What took place homosexually in Europe was infinitely more adventurous than what took place in America, as I've revealed in my books *German Homosexuality*, *French Homosexuality* and *Boarding School Homosexuality*.

In America homosexuality remained basically underground, although the American Revolution was greatly aided by the Prussian General von Steuben who counted among his lovers American boys of aristocratic backgrounds, including the son of the American president John Adams (2). Before the American Revolution buggery was a capital offense. After the Revolution sentences for sodomy were rapidly reduced from life sentences to brief imprisonment and fines.

In the 1920s gays went Hollywood (14), as the most beautiful among us do now, trying to break through as actors before accepting an incredible array of other jobs when they can't advance in acting careers, from studio grips to pool boys. Those who had succeeded had most often started out as hustlers, and as they aged they took on hustlers, the story of which is fully covered in my X-rated book *HUSTLERS*.

In 1924 Henry Gerber (1892 – 1972), born in Bavaria, immigrated to Chicago where he started the first quasi-secret homosexual society in America. At age 21, when war broke out with Germany, he was given the choice of being interned or of joining the American Army. He chose the Army and was sent to Coblenz for three years as a printer and proofreader. It was there he learned about Hirschfeld, the German homosexual sexologist, and became his acolyte, adopting, alas, Hirschfeld's idea that homosexuals were just naturally effeminate (2). Back in the States he worked at the post office in Chicago. He founded the first homosexual organization in America, the Society of Human Rights, the goal of which was: ''to promote and protect the interests of people who by reasons of mental and physical abnormalities are abused and hindered in the legal pursuit of happiness which is guaranteed them by the Declaration of Independence.'' As homosexuals were the ''mental and physical abnormalities'' he defended, we can be grateful for the fact that the Society had an early death, in a way that was almost hilarious: He decided to limit the Society to exclusively homosexuals (we don't know why), apparently unaware that his vice-president had two children. The vice-president's wife called the police who put Gerber on trial *three times* for being a degenerate. The charges were eventually dismissed but Gerber lost his life savings in lawyers' fees and the bribes it was necessary to pay out at the time (it being, after all, Chicago). He was fired from the post office for ''conduct unbecoming....''

He met up with an old army pal who suggested he reenlist, which he did, preparing magazines and recruiting publications for the Army Recruiting Bureau. He retired in 1945 and for the next thirty years was an active part of the N.Y. gay scene, also corresponding with groups around the country and in Germany. He entered the Soldiers' and Airmen's Home in Washington D.C. where he died at age 80 in 1972.

Although not a single rich Chicago homosexual offered Gerber a penny for his defense during his trial, they've made up for it since then. The Henry Gerber House where he had started the Society of Human Rights became an official Chicago Landmark in 2001 and then a National Historic Landmark just four years ago, in 2015. Gerber was enrolled in the Chicago Gay and Lesbian Hall of Fame, far too late for him to reap the rewards for his courage.

THE MATTACHINE SOCIETY
1950
Harry Hay - Dale Jennings, - Rudi Gernreich - James Gruber – Stonewall Riots – Gay Prides Parades – Radical Faerie – NAMBLA – Oreste Pucciani

Began in 1950, the Mattachine Society was named after masked French troubadours who wondered from village to village offering ballads that often-demanded social justice, although they also dealt with chivalry and courtly love, as well as occasional vulgar satires.

Mattachine meetings became popular because they were the first instances when men could come together and openly discuss their problems. The Society declined around 1961 because, conservative in nature, it misjudged the gay militancy that led to the

Stonewall Riots of 1969 (which in turn has led to today's street gatherings in San Francisco where boys can publicly suck and fuck, and the police had just better keep out of the way!).

Members of the Mattachine Society: Harry Hay (upper left), then (left to right) Konrad Stevens, Dale Jennings, Rudi Gernreich, Stan Witt, Bob Hull, Chuck Rowland (in glasses), Paul Bernard. Photo by James Gruber.

The Society was easily attackable because the founder, Harry Hay, had been a member of the Communist Party and was therefore a potential security risk. The McCarthy era was an anti-communist pogrom, the repercussions of which continue to our own day where a socialist candidate for the presidency (2016) is assailed as being a Communist. As homosexuality was not permitted within the Party, Hay was let go, although declared ''a Lifelong Friend of the People'' for past services. Other sources claim that it was Hay himself who resigned, although both events-- being expulsed and voluntarily quitting--could have conceivably taken place more or less concomitantly.

Hay toyed with naming the Society The Call, a call to form a fraternal organization based on protecting and bettering the members, but certainly not as a way, claimed Hay, of meeting boyfriends, although Hay succumbed immediately to the charms of Rudi Gernreich (his arm on Hay's knee in photo), his new lover. The first meeting took place in L.A. and among the first members were lovers Bob Hull and Chuck Rowland, Konrad Stevens, Dale Jennings and James Gruber (who dreamed up the name Mattachine Society, in preference to Hay's The Call, as well as Bachelors Anonymous, that Hay conceived along the lines of Alcoholics Anonymous [!]). Details of the lives of some of these men follow.

The Society was secret, with its oaths, secret words, secret handshake, five levels of membership, the whole organized like Communist cells. The aim was to unify isolated homosexuals and to help victimized gays.

In 1952 Jennings was arrested in a park for soliciting an undercover cop in a lewd manner. The Society maintained that the police had organized an entrapment and the ensuing trial was deadlocked. This was, for the Society, a perfect example of abuse, the very reason they had chosen the name of masked troubadours who, in medieval times, had risen up against lawless, repressive nobles. Entrapment had been used by the police for years, the sites being bars, parks and restrooms. Jennings was the first to *not* plead guilty and pay a fine, the others, all the others, having done so through fear of scandal. A playwright and novelist, and a veteran of W.W. II, Jennings was combative by nature and didn't fear the 10-day trial that followed, deadlocked 11-1 in favor of acquittal, which led to the dismissal of the charges.

Along the line Society members created, in 1953, the magazine *ONE*, one of whose founders was Jennings, published in the basement of Jennings' brother-in-law. It was seized for obscene filth that the U.S. Supreme Court exonerated in a unanimous decision, stating that there was nothing inherently filthy in a publication that discussed homosexuality. The circulation was small but the impact large. It was especially vociferous against police harassment. After leaving *ONE*, Jennings wrote a book, the homoerotic *Cowboys*, turned into a 1972 film starring John Wayne, giving Jennings enough money to buy a ranch, a ranch he later lost in a lawsuit brought by a former lover. Jennings died at age 82 in 2000.

After the trials and the publicity they occasioned, Society members gradually came out of the closet. But more conservative elements took control, denouncing the Communist past of Hay and declaring that members were imminently loyal Americans.

As stated, these were times when homosexuals were becoming more militant and far less conservative than Mattachine members, especially in N.Y. Those in California were infinitely tamer, due to their access to all the boys they wanted, busloads coming in daily, drawn by the film industry, in the Petri-dish paradise where the conditions--social, economic and weather-- were perfect, and during long nights alongside pools, boys could skinny dip and share their eroticism with likewise oriented friends, friends who didn't care to rock the boat as much as New Yorkers. A situation that exists today among actors in Hollywood where men marry in order to better mask the true targets of their lust, and as their wives are themselves often bisexual or lesbian, no one is harmed.

Briefly stated, the Mattachine Society fought against the injustice of labeling homosexuals a deviant group, discriminated against as are blacks and Jews, all of whom simply aspire to lead a life of their own choosing, so long as they do not infringe on the rights of others.

Henry ''Harry'' Hay (1912-2002) was born to an upper-middle-class American family in England, and traveled a great deal thanks to his father, a mining engineer, who beat him, perhaps, thought Hay, because he was slightly effeminate.

His first homosexual activity began at age 9 with a boy of 12 (the same age Byron, 9, discovered sex with his nanny) and at age 11 he discovered Carpenter's *The Intermediate Sex* (1) and the word homosexual (2), immediately recognizing his true nature. He flowered at L.A. High School, becoming president of the debating club and theater society, plus joining the R.O.T.C. He decided to prolong his high school experience by two years, remaining a total of five, although how he did so remains (to me) a mystery.

Hay

At age 10 he joined a boys' club, the Western Rangers, where he met Native Indians, the study of which became a life-long passion. He worked on a cousin's ranch where bunkhouse hands told him about men killed for trying to touch other men (a *Brokeback Mountain* reality), and at age 14 he was hired to work on a cargo ship, stating he was 21. He had sex with a 25-year-old sailor who filled him in on the ''secret brotherhood'' of global homosexuality. Along the way he gave up his mother's Catholicism and became a socialist before entering the Communist Party.

He attended Stanford at age 18 and from then on was an active participant in the gay scene, trying out everything sexual that came his way. He became *persona non grata* when he told a few select friends he was gay, which may have caused him to drop out of school two years in. Through gay friends he did a variety of jobs, in radio, as an understudy, a screen extra, a voice coach and a ghost-writer, all the time benefiting from sex that could include actors looking for a rapid blowjob to grips wanting someone for a quick fuck. He himself was taken on as a stuntman for some B movies, always a key post for men looking for ''real men'', more reasons, added to those I've already given, why the Hollywood region has been a homosexual paradise since the arrival of DeMille. Hay met and mated with actor Will Geer, a leftist who introduced him to the Communist Party, in which he became so invested he wound up giving courses in Marxism.

Will Geer

At age 25 he began analysis and, perhaps due to societal pressures, he swallowed analysts' convictions that he could become heterosexual by marring a boyish girl. He did so and the couple moved to N.Y. where Hay had a seven-month affair with architect William Alexander, as well as being one of the participants in Kinsey's sexual research, ending in the Kinsey Report. (Perhaps when one becomes satiated with sex, drugs and California boys-in-the-sand, Hollywood becomes far less paradisiacal.)

He returned to L.A. where he held an incredible array of jobs, par for the course for California boys, from salesman in a record shop to TV repairman. He divorced in 1950 after adopting two daughters he deeply loved and cared for. At age 50 he met a Danish hat maker, Jorn Kamgren, with whom he remained eleven years and helped establish thanks to Hay's Hollywood contacts.

Hay met inventor John Burnside with whom he finished his life. The Stonewall Riots of '69 left them both cold because they felt they had done far more already in forwarding gay rights in California. Two years earlier the police had infiltrated the Black Cat in L.A. and arrested men for kissing. When they refused to be led away like sheep they were beaten. This engendered an uproar in a nearby bar, New Faces, where the woman owner and two bartenders were knocked unconscious by the police. A march was organized with perhaps 200 people, but Californians had too much to gain in letting sleeping dogs lie to raise a real fuss.

It was the time of the counter-culture revolution, and both Hay and Burnside took to wearing colorful clothing, earrings, necklaces and their hair long. They picketed homophobic organizations and staged Gay-ins in Griffith Park, a homosexual *consommation-sur-place* zone.

Hay

     They moved to New Mexico where Hay could continue his interest in Indian cultures and encourage the gay community there. They initiated Albuquerque's first Gay Pride Parade in 1977. Aided by a few others, they organized a spiritual conference they called "a faerie" in Benson Arizona, attended by 220 men who left their clothes by the wayside in favor of feathers, beads, bells and rainbow makeup, where one learned about nutrition, giving massages and auto-fellatio (!).

A grouping of Faerie members: easy sex
of less than
Bel Ami physical quality.

Hay chose the name Radical Faerie for his new ''movement'' because Faerie made one think of both ''the immortal animistic spirit'' and of fairy, the slang word for gays. *He* refused to add the word ''movement'', stating that a faerie was a way of life. Hay declared himself a gay shaman, and the Radical Faerie was indeed built on paganism and anarchism, accompanied by environmentalism which added a note of cachet, but basically it was gays among gays, as naked as they wished, happy, camp and as opposed as possible to ''straight'' anything, where men cared for each other and sexuality was unbridled.

A second Faerie gathering was organized in 1980 near Boulder Colorado that was twice as big and long as the first. Hay was the feature speaker at the San Francisco Gay Pride Parade in 1982, Grand Marshal of the Long Beach Parade of 1986, and was invited to speak in the Sorbonne in Paris, an invitation he turned down.

He protested against the exclusion of the North American Man/Boy Love Association (NAMBLA), stating that "If the parents and friends of gays are truly friends of gays, they would know from their gay kids that the relationship with an older man is precisely what thirteen-, fourteen-, and fifteen-year-old kids need more than anything else in the world," certainly in remembrance of the sailor of 25 he had loved when he was 14.

The NAMBLA is a pedophile advocacy organization in the U.S. that works to abolish the age-of-consent laws and free men jailed for having consensual sex with minors. It keeps a very low profile for fear of police infiltration and the resultant imprisonment. One 1977 raid on a Boston suburb brought the arrest of twenty-four men who had used drugs and video games to lure boys into sexual acts the men filmed. In 1991 Mike Echols infiltrated the NAMBLA and wrote a book, *I Know my First Name is Steven,* absolutely heartbreaking:

In 1972 Steven Stayner, 5 years old, was kidnapped by Kenneth Parnell who immediately sexually molested the boy to whom he said his parents had given him away because they already had too many children, 5 including Steven. Steven remained with Parnell until age 14, free to come and go as he wished, changing schools as Parnell moved about California, at which time Parnell, wanting a younger boy, kidnapped 5-year-old Timothy White. It was because of White's screams that Steven took him to the police. Arrested, Parnell was accused of kidnapping but not of molesting the boys, a decision that protected them from the ''damaged goods'' label. Parnell was sentenced to 7 years but was out in 5, this just one of previous convictions before the Stayner abduction. The tragedy continued with Steven's death at age 24 from a motorcycle accident, Timothy a pallbearer at his funeral. Timothy himself perished at age 35 from a pulmonary embolism. He left behind two children, as did Steven. Both worked with abduction groups, speaking to children about the dangers of becoming involved with strangers. Parnell had destroyed Steven's life, a lad who never adjusted and found peace only in the grave. Child abusers are often themselves stalked by citizen groups, the story of Steven and Timothy the obvious reason why this is the case.

Despised by most of the gay community, NAMBLA defends itself by stating that ''man/boy love is by definition homosexual ... in the Western tradition from Socrates to Wilde to Gide.'' In reality, men who preyed on youths in Athens were put to death (4); Wilde was jailed; and Gide paid for his sex by giving coins to starving Arabs, a man as disgusting as are yesteryears' and today's priests who use the sanctity of the collar to collar children, collars rightly labeled as ''dog''.

A suit was brought against NAMBLA in 2000 when two men, after consulting the website, had stalked, tortured and murdered a boy (in 1997).

When a number of gay associations repudiated the site because, among other things, it sold ''The Rape and Escape Manual,'' Hay, in protest, wore a sign in the

1986 gay march in L.A.: ''NAMBLA walks with me.'' Allen Ginsberg, a member of NAMBLA, defended the organization by saying, ''I'm a member of NAMBLA because I love boys too--everybody does.'' There is even a Pedophilia Pride Day.

Cavorting nude in their Faerie, debauching underage boys and wallowing in public sucking and fucking, are a long, long way from the ideals of an ancient Greek culture Hay, Ginsberg, *et al* use as a cover, a perversion that would quite rightly make the lords of the Sacred Band vomit.

The conferences, organizations and other parades Hay participated in are incalculable, and have earned him the title, in some quarters, of the father of Gay Liberation--hopefully a joke concerning this person who started out with a great idea and finished up worthless garbage at age 90 in 2002.

Rudi Gernreich (1922-1985), Hay's lover, engaged in women's fashions, even though he remembers, as a boy, dreaming of ''leather chaps with a strap running between the buttocks of street laborers'', miles away from clothes for girls.

Rudi

At age 16 he and his mother, Jews, escaped from Austria to America where he did a number of odd jobs before designing women's clothing for different firms. He came out with his own line of clothing and immediately broke two taboos, both of which earned him money: he sold his creations to chain stores (as opposed to chic and expensive boutiques for the rich) and he invented unisex clothes. He then invented swimsuits with built-in bras and thought up, in 1964, the first monokini, making even bras outmoded. He made the cover of *TIME* in 1967. Next came see-through blouses, and leotards. When L.A. banned nude bathing in 1974 he invented thong bathing suits that displayed men and women's buttocks. He followed this with the pubikini, a window in the bathing suit showing men's and women's sculpted pubic hair (no picture available of the male version). Dresses with plunging fronts and backs followed.

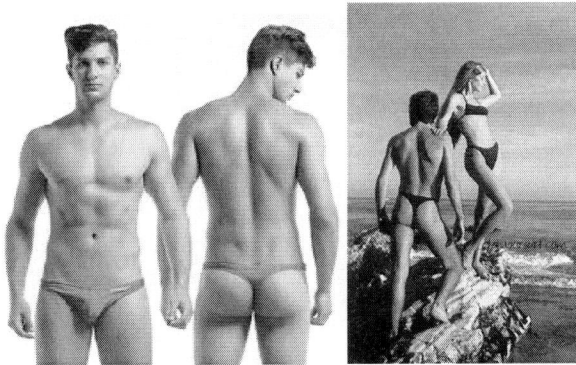

Thong swimwear

He ended his relationship with Hay in 1952. Personally, he wore jumpsuits and Gucci loafers. He died at age 62 from smoking, and he and his lover of 31 years, Oreste Pucciani, endowed a trust in their names for the American Civil Liberties Union. Pucciani graduated summa cum laude and Phi Beta Kappa from Adelbert College and took a doctorate in Romance languages from Harvard. He translated Racine's *Phèdre* and taught courses on Sartre at UCLA. He wrote a textbook *Langue et Langage* that underlined the merits of total immersion when learning a foreign tongue.

The N.Y. Metropolitan Museum of Art contains 100 of Gernreich's creations. A far more fulfilling ending than for Hay.

The lives of the other members of the society basically consisted of internal dissention between liberals and conservatives, and the musical beds of lovers changing lovers. An example: Chuck Rowland was deeply involved in *ONE* and invented its slogan, ''a mystic bond of brotherhood makes all men one.'' But due to Rowland's lack of respect for *ONE*'s leadership his resignation was accepted, even though he hadn't submitted it. Rowland then founded his own church, behind which he could organize gays protected by the First Amendment. The church folded and he got a masters and a teaching job in a high school in Iowa. In 1982 he founded the Celebration Theater in L.A., dedicated to gay works. The theater had its ups-and-downs but he found himself among friends, ''the best months of my life'' he said, just before he died, in 1990. Along the way Bob Hull committed suicide, at the end of nearly life-long depression, stated his last lover.

The full history of the Mattachine Society can be found in my book of that name (15).

SOURCES

1- See my book *Boarding School Homosexuality*.
2- See my book *German Homosexuality*.
3- See my book *TROY*.
4- See my book *Greek Homosexuality*.
5- See my book *SPARTA*.
6- See my book *John (Jack) Nicholson*.
7- See my book *Homosexual Warriors*.
8- See my book *The Bloomsbury Set*.
9- See my book *Phallus*.
10- See my book *Rent Boys*.
11- See my book *Menshikov*.
12- See my book *ARGO*.
13- See my book *Omnisexuality*.
14- See my book *The Garden of Allah*.
15- See my book *Mattachine Society*.
16- See my Alexander and Hephaestion.
17- See my book *Hadrian and Antinous*.

The major Greek and Roman Sources consulted in the writing of this book:

Aelianus was a Roman author and teacher of rhetoric who spoke and wrote in Greek.

Aeschylus, of whom 7 out of perhaps 90 plays have survived. His gravestone celebrated his heroism during the victory against the Persians at Marathon and *not his plays*, proof of the extraordinary importance of Greek survival against the barbarians (sadly, he lost his brother at Marathon). He is said to have been a deeply religious person, dedicated to Zeus. As a boy he worked in a vineyard until Dionysus visited him in a dream and directed him to write plays. One of his plays supposedly divulged too much about the Eleusinian Mysteries and he was nearly stoned to death by the audience. He had to stand trial but pleaded ignorance. He got off when the judges learned of the death of his brother at Marathon and when Aeschylus showed the wounds he and a second brother had received at Marathon too, the second brother left with but a stump in place of his hand. In one of his later plays Pericles was part of the chorus. The subjects of his plays often concerned Troy and the Persian Wars, Marathon, Salamis and Xerxes (Xerxes is accused of losing the war due to hubris; his building of the bridge over the Hellespont was a show of arrogance the gods found unacceptable). In *Seven against Thebes* he relates the destinies of Oedipus' two sons who agree to become kings of Thebes on alternate years. Naturally, when the time comes for them to change places the king in place refuses, which leads to both boys killing each other. *Agamemnon* is an excellent retelling of the Trojan War, as Agamemnon sails home to be murdered by his wife Clytemnestra. In *The Libation Bearers* Agamemnon's boy Orestes returns home to destroy his father's assassins, Clytemnestra and her lover Aegisthus. In *The Eumenides* (the Kindly Spirits) Orestes is chased by the Furies for having killed his mother. He takes shelter with Apollo who decides, with Athena, to try the boy before a court. The vote is a tie, but Athena, preaching the importance of reason and understanding, acquits him. She then changes the terrible Furies into sweet Eumenides.

Anacreon was born in 582 B.C. and was known for his drinking songs.

Andocides was implicated in the Hermes scandal and saved his skin by turning against Alcibiades in a speech that has come down to us called, what else?, *Against Alcibiades*.

Appian, who lived during the reigns of Trajan and Hadrian, was a Roman historian of Greek origin. He was a friend of Fronto, Marcus Aurelius' tutor and, perhaps, lover. He left his book, *Roman History*, which describes, among other events, the Roman civil wars.

Aristophanes, my preferred playwright, is, naturally, the father of comedy. He wrote perhaps 40 plays of which 11 remain. He was feared by all: Plato states that it was his play *The Clouds* the root of the trial that cost Socrates his life. Nearly nothing is known about him other than what he himself revealed in his works. Playwrights were obliged to be conservative because part of each play was funded by a wealthy citizen, an honor for the citizen and a caveat for the author. He was an exponent of make-love-not-war who saw his country go from its wonderful defeat of the Persians to its end at the hands of the Spartans. Along with Alcibiades and Socrates, Aristophanes is featured in Plato's *The Symposium* in which he is gently mocked, proof that he was considered, even by those he poked fun at, as affable. *The Acharnians* highlights the troubles the Athenians went through after the death of Pericles and their defeat at the hands of Sparta. *The Peace* focuses on the Peace of Nicias. *Lysistrata* tells about the plight of women trying to bring about peace in order to prevent the sacrifice of their sons during war, occasioning the world's first sex strike. When Athens lost its freedom to Sparta, Aristophanes stopped writing plays.

<u>Athenaeus</u> lived in the times of Marcus Aurelius. His *Deipnosopistae* is a banquet conversation *à la Platon* during which conversations on every possible subject takes place, filling fifteen books that have come down to us.

<u>Ausonius</u> was a Latin poet and teacher of rhetoric, around 350 B.C.

<u>Bion</u> was a Greek philosopher known for his diatribes, satires and attacks on religion. He lived around 300 B.C.

<u>Cassius Dio</u>, 155 A.D. to 235 A.D., was a noted historian who wrote in Greek and published a history of Rome in 80 volumes, many of which have survived, giving modern historians a detailed look into his times.

<u>Cicero</u> was born in 106 B.C. and murdered by Mark Antony in 43 B.C. Michael Grant said it all when he wrote, ''the influence of Cicero upon the history of European

literature and ideas greatly exceeds that of any other prose writer in any language."

Cornelius Nepos was a Roman friend of Cicero. Most of what he wrote was lost, so what we know comes through passages of his works in the books of other historians.

Ctesias was a Greek historian from Anatolian Caria, and the physican of Artaxerxes, whom he accompanied in his war against his brother Cyrus the Younger. He wrote a book on India, *Indica* and Persia, *Persica*. The fragments we have of his writing come to us through Diodorus Siculus and Plutarch.

Diodorus Siculus lived around 50 B.C. and wrote *Historical Library*, consisting of forty volumes.

Diogenes of Sinope (aka Diogenes the Cynic) comes to use through extracts of his writing passed on by others, as nothing he wrote has survived. He had a truly remarkable life, at first imprisoned for debasing the coins his father, a banker, minted. Afterwards he pled poverty, sleeping in a huge ceramic jar, walking the streets of Athens during the day with a lighted lamp, saying he was in search of an honest man, and teasing Plato by noisily eating through his lectures (later Plato claimed he was "a Socrates gone mad".) On a voyage he was captured and sold as a slave in Crete to a Corinthian who was so entranced by his intelligence that he made him his sons' teacher. It was in his master's household that he grew old and died. Plutarch tells us he met Alexander the Great while Diogenes was staring at a pile of bones. In answer to Alexander's question he said he was searching for the bones of Alexander's father, but could not distinguish them from those of a slave. Alexander supposedly said that if he couldn't be Alexander he would choose to be Diogenes. He was the first man ever to claim to be "a citizen of the world." He urinated on people, defecated where he would and masturbated in public, about which he said, "If only I could banish hunger by rubbing my belly." The word cynic meant dog-like, and when someone questioned him about it he said he too was dog-like because he licked those who helped him, barked at those who didn't, and bit his enemies. Rogers and Hart wrote these lyrics about him: There was an old zany/who lived in a tub; he had so many flea-bites/he didn't know where to rub.

Eupolis lived around 430 B.C. An Athenian poet who wrote during the Peloponnesian Wars.

Euripides may have written 90 plays of which 18 survive. His approach was a study of the inner lives of his personages, the predecessor of Shakespeare. Due to his stance on certain subjects, he thought it best to leave Athens voluntarily rather than suffer an end similar to that of Socrates. An example: ''I would prefer to stand three times to confront my enemies in battle rather than bear a single child!'' He was born on the island of Salamis, of Persian-War fame; in fact he was born on the very day of the battle. His youth was spent in athletics and dance. Due to bad marriages with unfaithful wives, he withdrew to Salamis where he wrote while contemplating sea and sky. When Sparta defeated Athens in war, it did not burn the city to the ground: Plutarch states that this was thanks to one of Euripides' plays, *Electra*, put on for the Spartans in Athens, a play they found so wonderful that they proclaimed that it would be barbarous to destroy a city capable of engendering men of the quality of Euripides. (The real reason was to preserve the city that had twice saved Greece from Persian victory.) Euripides was known for his love of Agathon, a youth praised for his beauty as well as for his culture, and would later become a playwright. Aristophanes mocked Euripides for loving Agathon long after he had left his boyhood behind him. (Remember, not everyone followed boy-love to the letter. The idea of men loving boys until they grew whiskers did not always hold true. Boys grown ''old'' could shave their chins and butts; some men just preferred other men, hairy or not, while most men impregnated boys but other men adored being penetrated.) Plato says that Agathon had polished manners, wealth, wisdom and dispensed hospitality with ease and refinement.

<u>Herodian</u> wrote a history of Greece entitled *History of the Empire from the Death of Marcus*, in eight books. Thanks to him we learn a great deal about Elagabalus.

<u>Herodotus</u> was contemporary to some of the events that interest us here. Cicero called him the Father of History, while Plutarch wrote that he was the Father of Lies. His masterpiece is *The Histories*, considered a chef-d'oeuvre, a work that the gods have preserved intact right up to our own day, a divine intervention that would not have

surprised a believer like Herodotus (it's also a book I reread every year). Part of his work may have been derived from other sources (what historian's work isn't?) and the facts rearranged in an effort to give them dramatic force and please an audience. Much of what he did was based on oral histories, many of which themselves were based on early folk tales, highly suspect, naturally, in all their details. Aristophanes made fun of segments of his work and Thucydides called Herodotus a storyteller. Surprisingly little is known about his own life. For example, he writes lovingly about Samos, leading some to believe that he may have spent his youth there. Born near Ionia, he wrote in that dialect, learning it perhaps on Samos. He was his own best publicist, taking his works to festivals and games, such as the Olympic Games, and reading them to the spectators. As I've said, many people doubt that he actually went where he said he went and saw what he said he saw. But the same was true of Marco Polo who causes disbelief to this day simply because he never mentioned eating noodles in China or seeing the Great Wall or even drinking Chinese tea. No historian, then as now, can write a book on ancient occurrences without referring to Herodotus' observations. An amusing example of recent discoveries that give credence to Herodotus is this: Herodotus wrote about a kind of giant ant, the size of a fox, living in India, in the desert, that dug up gold. This was ridiculed until the French ethnologist Peissel came upon a marmot living in today's Pakistan that burrows in the sand and has for generations brought wealth to the region by bringing up gold from its burrows. Peissel suggests that the original confusion came from the fact that the Persian word for marmot was similar to the word for mountain ant.

<u>Isocrate</u> was a student of Socrates who wrote a speech in the defense of Alcibiades during a trial that took place after his death.

<u>Josephus</u>, 37 A.D. to around 100 A.D., was a historian born in Jerusalem. He fought against the Romans and was captured by Vespasian who kept him as his interpreter and, later, Josephus even assumed the emperor's family name, becoming a citizen (Titus Flavius Josephus). A Jew, he turned against his people and helped Vespasian's son Titus to loot the Second Temple. His works include *The Jewish War* and *Antiquities of the Jews.*

Juvenal was a satirical poet who wrote *Satires*.

Lucan (Marcus Annaeus Lucanus) lived from 39 A.D. to 65 A.D., a short life due to his being ordered by Nero to commit suicide because of his role in the treasonous Piso conspiracy. In hopes of a pardon, he implicated his mother among others, all of whom followed him in death. He was a poet, a close friend of Nero until the emperor grew tired of him and his poetry, after which Lucan's writing became insulting, insults Nero was said to have ignored.

Lysias was extremely wealthy and contemporary with Alcibiades. He founded a new profession, logographer, which consisted of writing speeches delivered in law courts. One of his speeches was *Against Andocides*, another was *Against Alcibiades*.

Memmius was an orator and poet, and friend of Pompey but eventually went over to Caesar.

Mimnermus was born in Ionian Smyrna around 630 B.C. He wrote short love poems suitable for performance at drinking parties.

Myron of Priene is the author of a historical account of the First Messenian War.

Pausanias, a Greek historian and geographer, famous for his *Description of Greece*. He was contemporary with Hadrian and Marcus Aurelius. He's noted as being someone interested in everything, careful in his writing and scrupulously honest.

Phanocles lived during the time of Alexander the Great. He was the author of a poem on boy-love that described the love of Orpheus for Calais, and his death at the hands of Thracian women.

Philemon lived to be a hundred but alas only fragments of his works remain. He must have been very popular as he won numerous victories as a poet and playwright.

Pindar's great love was Theoxenus of Tenodos about whom he wrote: ''Whosoever, once he has seen the rays flashing from the eyes of Theoxenus, and is not shattered by the waves of desire, has a black heart forged of a cold flame. Like wax of the sacred bees, I melt when I look at the young limbs of boys.'' He lived around 500 B.C. and celebrated the Greek victories against the Persians at Salamis and Plataea. His home in Thebes became a must for his devotees.

Plato was a major source for this book, along with Xenophon, Thucydides and

Plutarch. Plato's most famous work is the Allegory of the Cave. Humans in the cave have no other reality than the shadows they see on the walls. If they looked around, they could see what was casting the shadows and by doing so gain additional knowledge. If they left the cave they would discover the sun, analogous to truth. If those who saw the sun reentered the cave and told the others, they would not be believed. There are thusly different levels of reality that only the wisest are able to see; the others remain ignorant. It's basically thanks to Plato and Xenophon that we know what we do about Socrates. Plato's perfect republic is ruled by the best (an aristocracy), headed by a philosopher king who guides his people thanks to his wisdom and reason. An inferior form of government, one that comes after an aristocracy, is a timocracy, ruled by the honorable. A timocracy is in the hands of a warrior class. Plato has Sparta in mind, but it's unclear how he could have found this form of government better than, for example, a democracy. The problem may be that we know, in reality, so little about Sparta. Next comes an oligarchy based on wealth, followed by a democracy, rule by just anyone and everyone. This degenerates into a tyranny, meaning a government of oppression, because of the conflict between the rich and the poor in a democracy.

Pliny the Younger was the Elder's nephew. He witnessed the explosion of Vesuvius. He was a lawyer and a letter writer, many of which remain, vital historical sources of the times. His letters concerning Trajan are of special importance. Under Trajan he worked side by side with Suetonius.

Plutarch was born near Delphi around 46 A.D. to a wealthy family. He was married, and a letter to his wife even exists to this day. He had sons, the exact number unknown. He studied mathematics and philosophy in Athens and was known to have visited most of the major Greek sites mentioned in this book, as well as Rome. He personally knew the Emperors Trajan and Hadrian, and became a Roman citizen. He was a high priest at Delphi and his duty consisted of interpreting the auguries of the Pythoness (no mean task). He wrote the *Lives of the Emperors* but alas only two of the lesser emperors survive. Another verily monumental work was *Parallel Lives of Greeks and Romans* of which twenty-three exist. His interest was the destinies of his subjects, how they made their way through the meanders of life, the Jekyll/Hyde struggle of virtue versus vice. A small jest, he went on, often reveals more than battles during which thousands die. His writings on Sparta, alongside those of Xenophon, are nearly all we possess concerning that extraordinary city-state. His major biographies are the *Life of Alexander* and the *Life of Julius Caesar*. Amusingly, Plutarch wrote a scathing review of Herodotus' work in which he stated that the great historian was fanatically biased in favor of the Greeks who could do, according to Herodotus, no wrong.

No gratitude can ever be enough for what this man has given us, although in the case of the Greeks we must never forget that he was writing *500 years after the events.*

Polybius, around 200 B.C. to 118 B.C., was a Greek historian whose *The Histories* covered the period from 264 to 146 B.C. He was a friend of Scipio Africanus. He details the ascent to empire of Rome, and was present at the destruction of Carthage.

Polyenus was a Macedonian known as a rhetorician and for his books on war strategies.

Sallust was a Roman historian and politician, 86 B.C. to about 35 B.C. One of his works concerned Catiline and he wrote *Histories* of which only fragments remain.

Seneca (Lucius Annaeus Seneca) lived around 4 B.C. to 65 A.D. He was the advisor of Caligula, Claudius and Nero who forced him to commit suicide for supposedly planning his overthrow. He is known for his philosophical essays, letters and tragedies.

Simonides of Ceos was a Greek poet born about 550 B.C. Besides his poems, he added four letters to the Greek alphabet.

Suetonius (Gaius Suetonius Tranquillus) lived around 69 A.D. to 123 A.D. He was a truly great Roman historian known for his *Twelve Caesars*, his only extant work. Pliny the Younger says that he was studious and totally dedicated to writing. He was highly favored by both Trajan, under whom he served as his secretary, and Hadrian who fired him for having an affair with the Empress Vibia Sabina.

Sophocles was the author of 123 plays of which 7 remain, notably *Oedipus* and *Antigone*. An Athenian born to a rich family just before the Battle of Marathon, he was a firm supporter of Pericles. He fought alongside Pericles against Samos when the island attempted to become autonomous from Athens. He was elected as a magistrate during the Sicilian Expedition led by Alcibiades, and given for function the goal of finding out why the expedition had ended disastrously. Sophocles was always ready and willing to succumb to the charms of boys. Plutarch tells us that even at age 65 ''Sophocles led a handsome boy outside the city walls to have his way with him. He spread the boy's poor himation--a rectangular piece of cloth thrown over the left shoulder that drapes the body-- upon the ground. To cover them both he spread his rich cloak. After Sophocles took his pleasure the boy took the cloak and left the himation for Sophocles. This misadventure was eventually known to all.'' He died at 90, some say while reciting a very long tirade from *Antigone* because he hadn't paused to take a breath. Another version has him choking on grapes, and a final one has him dying of happiness after winning the equivalent of our Oscar at a festival. The first of his trilogy--called the Theban plays--is *Oedipus the King*. Here the baby Oedipus--in a plot that goes back to Priam and Paris at the founding of Troy--is handed over to a servant to be killed in order to prevent the accomplishment of an oracle, an oracle stating that he will kill his father and marry his mother. He does both after solving the riddle of the sphinx (which creature becomes four-footed, then two-footed and finally three-footed?). His mother, when she finds out she's been bedding her own son, commits suicide and Oedipus blinds himself. In *Oedipus at Colonus* Oedipus dies and we learn more about his children Antigone, Polyneices and Eteocles. In *Antigone* Polyneices is accused of treason and killed. His body is thrown outside the city walls and the king forbids its burial, under pain of death. Antigone does so anyway and, faced with death, she commits suicide, followed by the king's son who was going to wed her, followed by the king's wife who couldn't face losing her precious son. (Whew!)

Tacitus, around 56 A.D. to 117 A.D., was a historian who wrote *Annals* and *Histories*, concerning Tiberius, Claudius, Nero and the Year of the Four Emperors. He is known for his insights into the psychology of his subjects.

Theocritus was a Sicilian and lived around 270 B.C. In his 7th Idyll Aratus is passionately in love with a lad. His 12th Idyll refers to Diocles who died saving the life of

Philolaus, the boy he loved, and in whose honor kissing contests were held every spring at his tomb. In his 23rd Idyll a lover commits suicide because of unrequited love, warning his belovèd that one day he too will burn and weep for a cruel boy. Before hanging himself the lover kissed the doorpost from which he would attach the noose. The boy treated the corpse with disdain and went off to the gymnasium for a swim where a statue of Eros fell on him, coloring the water with his blood. In his 29th Idyll a lover warns his belovèd that he too will age and his beauty will lose its freshness. He is therefore advised to show more kindness as ''you will one day be desperate for a beautiful young man's attentions.'' Although lads are often disappointing, it is impossible not to fall madly in love with them. In the 30th Idyll the poet states that when a man grows old he should keep a distance from boys, but in his heart he knows that the only alternative to loving a boy is simply to cease to exist.

Theognis was born around 550 B.C. His poems consist of maxims and advice as to how to live life. Fortunately, a great deal of his work has come down to us, most of which is dedicated to his belovèd, the handsome Cyrnus.

<u>Thucydides</u> was an Athenian general and historian, contemporary with the events he described. What he wrote was based on what actually happened; there was no extrapolating; no divine intervention on the part of the gods as was the case with Plutarch. An example of this was his observation that birds and animals that ate plague victims died as a result, leading him to conclude that the disease had a natural rather than supernatural cause. His description of the plague has never been equaled, the plague that he himself caught while participating in the Peloponnesian War. He is thought to have died in 411 B.C., the date at which his writing suddenly stops. He admired Pericles and democracy but not the radical form found in Athens.

<u>Tyrtaeus</u>, a rare Spartan writer, left us an account of the Second Messenian War. The purpose of his poetry was to inspire Spartan support of the Spartan state. Athenians claimed he was of Athenian birth. Pausanias maintained that the Athenians had sent him to Sparta as an insult, because he was both crazy, lame and had one eye. Herodotus wrote

that he was only one of two foreigners to be given Spartan citizenship.

    <u>Xenophon</u>, born near Athens in 430 B.C., was a historian and general. His masterpieces are *The Peloponnesian Wars* and *Anabasis*. He loved Sparta and served under Spartan generals during the Persian Wars. Like the Spartans, he believed in oligarchic rule, rule by the few, be they the most intelligent or wealthy or militarily acute. He spent a great deal of time in Persia alongside Cyrus the Younger who raised an army, among whom were Xenophon's 10,000 and other mercenaries (all of which is the subject of *Anabasis*). After Cyrus' death Xenophon and his ten thousand made their way back home, the breathtaking account of which ends his *Anabasis*. The Athenians exiled him when he fought with the Spartans against Athens but the Spartans offered him an estate where he wrote his works. His banishment may have been revoked thanks to his son Gryllus who brilliantly fought and died for Athens.

OTHER SOURCES

Abbott Jacob, *History of Pyrrhus*, 2009.
Ady, Cecilia, *A History of Milan under the*

Sforza, 1907.

Aldrich and Wotherspoon, *Who's Who in Gay and Lesbian History*, 2001.

Aristophanes, Bantam Drama, 1962.

Baglione, *Caravaggio*, circa 1600.

Baker Simon, *Ancient Rome*, 2006.

Barber, Richard, *The Devil's Crown--Henry II and Sons*, 1978.

Barber, Stanley, *Alexandros*, 2010.

Bawlf, Samuel, *The Secret Voyage of Sir Francis Drake*, 2003.

Beachy, Robert, *Gay Berlin*, 2014. Marvelous.

Bellori, *Caravaggio*, circa 1600.

Bergreen, Laurence, *Over the Edge of the World. Magellan.* 2003.

Bicheno, Hugh, *Vendetta*, 2007.

Bierman, John, *Dark Safari, Henry Morton Stanley*, 1990.

Blanchard, Jean-Vincent, *Éminence, Cardinal Richelieu and the Rise of*

Boyd, Douglas, *April Queen*, 2004.

Boyles, David, *Blondel's Song*, 2005.

Bradford, Ernle, *Thermopylae*, 1980.

Bramly, Serge, *Leonardo*, 1988. A wonderful book.

Burg, B.R., *Gay Warriors*, 2002.

Burg, B.R., *Sodomy and the Pirate Tradition*, 1989.

Bury and Meiggs, *A History of Greece*, 1975.
Calimach, Andrew, *Lover's Legends*, 2002.
Carroll, Stuart, *Maryrs & Murderers, The Guise Family*, 2009.
Carry Peter, *True History of the Kelly Gang*, 2000.
Cartledge, Paul, *Alexander the Great*, 2004.
Cartledge, Paul, *Sparta and Lakonia*, 1979.
Cartledge, Paul, *The Spartans*, 2002.
Cartledge, Paul, *Thermopylae*, 2006.
Cate, Curtis, *Friedrich Nietzsche*, 2003.
Cawthorne, Nigel, *Sex Lives of the Popes*, 1996.
Cellini, Benvenuto, *The Autobiography of Benvenuto Cellini.*
Ceram, C.W., *Gods, Graves and Scholars*, 1951.
Chamberlin, E.R. *The Fall of the House of Borgia*, 1974.
Cloulas, Ivan, *The Borgia*, 1989
Conner, Clifford, *Jean Paul Marat*, 2012.
Cooper, John, *The Queen's Agent*, 2011.
Crompton, Louis, *Byron and Greek Love*, 1985.
Crompton, Louis, *Homosexuality and Civilization*, 2003.
Crouch, David, *William Marshal*, 1990.
Crowley, Roger, *Empires of the Sea*, 2008.

Marvelous.
Curtis Cate, *Friedrich Nietzsche*, 2002.
Davidson, James, *Courtesans and Fishcakes*, 1998.
Davidson, James, *The Greeks and Greek Love*, 2007.
Davis, John Paul, *The Gothic King, Henry III*, 2013.
Dover K.J. *Greek Homosexuality*, 1978
Eisler, Benita, *BYRON Child of Passion, Fool of Fame*, 2000. Wonderful.
Erlanger, Philippe, *Buckingham*, 1951.
Erlanger, Philippe, *The King's Minion*, 1901.
Everitt Anthony, *Augustus*, 2006.
Everitt Anthony, *Cicero*, 2001.
Everitt, Anthony, *Hadrian*, 2009.
Fagles, Robert, *The Iliad*, 1990.
Forellino, Antonio, *Michelangelo*, 2005. Beautiful reproductions.
Frieda, Leonie, *Catherine de Medici*, 2003. Wonderful.
Gayford, Martin, *Michelangelo*, 2013. A beautiful book.
Gillingham, John, *Richard the Lionheart*, 1978.
Goldsworthy Adrian, *Caesar*, 2006
Goldsworthy Adrian, *The Fall of Carthage*, 2000.

Goodman Rob and Soni Jimmy, *Rome's Last Citizen*, 2012.

Graham-Dixon, Andrew, *Caravaggio* 2010. Fabulous.

Grant Michael, *History of Rome*, 1978.

Graves, Robert, *Greek Myths*, 1955.

Gray, George, *The Children's Crusade*, (no date).

Guicciardini, *Storie fiorentine (History of Florence)*, 1509. Essential.

Halperin David M. *One Hundred Years of Homosexuality*, 1990

Harris Robert, *Imperium*, 2006.

Herodotus, *The Histories*, Penguin Classics.

Hesiod and Theognis, Penguin Classics, 1973.

Hibbert, Christopher, *Florence, the Biography of a City*, 1993.

Hibbert, Christopher, *The Borgias and Their Enemies*, 2009.

Hibbert, Christopher, *The Great Mutiny India 1857*, 1978. Fabulous.

Hibbert, Christopher, *The Rise and Fall of the House of Medici*, 1974.

Hicks, Michael, *Richard III*, 2000.

Hine, Daryl, *Puerilities*, 2001.

Hirst, Michael, *The Tudors*, 2007.

Hochschild, Adam, *King Leopold's Ghost*, 1999.

Holland Tom, *Rubicon*, 2003.

Holland, Tom, *Persian Fire*, 2005.

Hughes Robert, *Rome*, 2011.

Hughes-Hallett, *Heroes*, 2004.

Hughes, Robert, *Rome*, 2011.

Hughes, Robert, *The Fatal Shore*, 1987.

Jack Belinda, *Beatrice's Spell*, 2004.

James, Callum, *My Dear KJ...* edited by James, 2015.

Jeal, Tim, *Explorers of the Nile*, 2011. Wonderful.

Jeal, Tim, *STANLEY*, 2007. All of Jeal's books are must-reads.

Johnson, Marion, *The Borgias*, 1981.

Kagan, Donald, *The Peloponnesian War*, 2003.

Knecht, Robert, *The French Religious Wars 1562-98*, 2002.

Köhler, Joachim, *Zarathustra's Secret*, 1989.

Lacey, Robert, *Henry VIII*, 1972.

Lambert, Gilles *Caravaggio*, 2007.

Landucci, Luca, *A Florentine Diary*, around 1500, a vital source.

Lévy, Edmond, *Sparte, 1979.*

Lewis, Bernard, *The Assassins*, 1967.

Livy, *Rome and the Mediterranean*

Livy, *The War with Hannibal.*

Loomis, Stanley, *Paris in the Terror*, 1986.

Lubkin, Gregory, *A Renaissance Court*, 1994.

Lyons, Mathew, *The Favourite*, 2011.

Macintyre, Ben, *The Man Who Would Be King*, 2004.

Malye, Jean, *La Véritable Histore d'Alcibiade*, 2009.

Manchester, William, *A World Lit Only By Fire*, 1993.

Mancini, *Caravaggio*, circa 1600.

Marchand, Leslie, *Byron*, 1971.

Matyszak, Philip, *The Mithridates the Great*, 2008.

McLynn, Frank, *Richard and John, Kings of War*, 2007. Fabulous.

McLynn, *Marcus Aurelius*, 2009.

McLynn, *STANLEY, The making of an African explorer*, 1989.

Meier, Christian, *Caesar*, 1996.

Meyer, G.J. *The Borgias, The Hidden History*, 2013.

Meyer, G.J. *The Tudors*, 2010.

Meyer, Jack, *Alcibiades*, 2009.

Miles Richard, *Ancient Worlds*, 2010.

Miles Richard, *Carthage Must be Destroyed*, 2010.

Miller, David, *Richard the Lionheart*, 2003.

Moore Lucy, *Amphibious Thing*, 2000.

Moote, Lloyd, *Louis XIII, The Just*, 1989.

Mortimer, Ian, 1415, *Henry V's Year of Glory*,

2009.

Nelson, Craig, *Thomas Paine*, 2006.

Nicholl, Charles, *The Reckoning*, 2002.

Noel, Gerard, *The Renaissance Popes*, 2006.

Norton, Rictor, *My Dear Boy*, Love Letters edited by Norton, 1998.

Opper, Thorsten, *Hadrian, Empire and Conflict*, 2008.

Paladilhe, Dominique, *Le Prince de Condé*, 2005.

Parker, Derek, *Cellini*, 2003, the book is beautifully written.

Pascal, Jean Claude, *L'Amant du Roi*, 1991.

Payne, Robert and Nihita Romanoff, *Ivan the Terrible*, 2002.

Pearce, Joseph, *The Unmasking of Oscar Wilde*, 2000.

Pernot, Michel, *Henri III, Le Roi Décrié*, 2013, Excellent book.

Petitfils, Jean-Christian, *Louis XIII*, 2008, wonderful.

Plutarch's Lives, Modern Library.

Polybius, *The Histories*.

Porter, Darwin, *Howard Hughes*, 2010.

Read, Piers Paul, *The Templars*, 1999.

Reid, B.L., *The Lives of Roger Casement*, 1976.

Reston, James, *Warriors of God, Richard and the Crusades*, 2001.

Rice, Edward, *Captain Sir Richard Francis Burton*, 1990.

Ridley, Jasper, *The Tudor Age*, 1998.

Robb, Peter, M – *The Man Who Became Caravaggio*, 1998.

Rocco, Antonio, *Alcibiade Enfant à l'Ecole*, 1630.

Rocke, Michael, *Forbidden Friendships*, 1996. Fabulous/indispensible.

Romans Grecs et Latin, Gallimard, 1958.

Ross, Charles, *Richard III*, 1981.

Rouse, W.H.D., Homer's *The Iliad*, 1938.

Royle, Trevor, *Fighting Mac, The Downfall of Sir Hector Macdonald*.

Ruggiero, Guido, *The Boundaries of Eros*, 1985.

Sabatini, Rafael, *The Life of Cesare Borgia*, 1920.

Saint Bris, Gonzague, *Henri IV*, 2009.

Saslow, James, *Ganymede in the Renaissance*, 1986.

Schama, Simon, *Citizens* 1989.

Seward, Desmond, *Caravaggio – A Passionate Life*, 1998.

Shapiro, James, *1599*, 2005.

Simonetta, Marcello, *The Montefeltro Conspiracy*, 2008. Wonderful.

Skidmore, Chris, *Bosworth*, 1988.

Skidmore, Chris, *Death and the Virgin*, 2010.
Solnon, Jean-Fançois, *Henry III*, 1996.
Stewart, Alan, *The Cradle King, A Life of James VI & I*, 2003.
Stirling, Stuart, *Pizarro Conqueror of the Inca*, 2005.
Strathern, Paul, *The Medici, Godfathers of the Renaissance*, 2003. Superb.
Strauss Barry, *The Spartacus War*, 2009.
Stuart, Stirling, *Pizarro - Conqueror of the Inca*, 2005.
Suetonius, *The Twelve Caesars*.
Tacitus, *The Annals of Imperial Rome*.
Tacitus, *The Histories*.
Thucydides, *The Peloponnesian War*, Penguin Classics.
Tibullus, *The Elegies of Tibullus*, translated by Theodore C. Williams
Tuchman, Barbara, *A Distant Mirror*, 1978.
Turner, Ralph, *Eleanor of Aquitaine*, 2009.
Unger Miles, *Magnifico, The Brilliant Life and Violent Times*
Vernant, Jean-Pierre, *Mortals and Immortals*, 1991.
Virgil, *The Aeneid*, Everyman's Library, Knopf, 1907.
Viroli, Maurizio, *Niccolo's Smile, A Biography of Machiavelli*, 1998.

Ward-Perkins Bryan, *The Fall of Rome*, 2005
Warren, W.L., *Henry II*, 1973.
Weir, Alison, *Eleanor of Aquitaine*, 1999. Weir is a fabulous writer.
Wheaton James, *Spartacus*, 2011.
Whyte, Kenneth, *The Uncrowned King*, 2008.
Wikipedia: Research today is impossible without the aid of this monument.
Williams Craig A. *Roman Homosexuality*, 2010.
Williams John, *Augustus*, 1972.
Wilson, Derek, *The Uncrowned Kings of England*, 2005.
Worthington, Ian, *Philip II of Macedonia*, 2008.
Wright, Ed, *History's Greatest Scandals*, 2006.
Xenophon, *A History of My Time*s, Penguin Classics.
Xenophon, *The Persian Expedition*, 1949.
Zachks, Richard, *History Laid Bare*, 1994.

INDEX

Please note that the page numbers are *passim*. An example, Oscar Wilde 76 – 102 means that Wilde is found within these pages, but not necessarily on *every* page.

Attalus 97-146 *passim*
Bacchylides 97-146 *passim*
Bagg, Lyman 200
Balwin II 11
Band of Boys 65-78 *passim*
Batalos 97-146 *passim*
Bather, The 239
Batis, governor of Tyre 97-146 *passim*
Baybars 15
Beardsley, Aubrey 42-43
Becket, Thomas à 14
Bell, Julian 213
Bell, Vanessa 228-248 *passim*
Benedict XIII 16
Bergen, George 235-236
Bernard, Paul 254
Bikini 268-269
Black Cat 261
Blockhouse 65-78 *passim*
Bloomsbury Set *passim*
Blunt, Anthony 202-249 *passim*
Boers 65-78 *passim*
Bono, Andrea De 79-95 *passim*
Brokeback Mountain 159
Brooke, Rupert 224-228 *passim*
Brookfield, Frances 205
Browne, Denis 224-228 *passim*
Browning, Oscar 209

Bucephalas 97-146 *passim*
Burgess, Guy 202-249 *passim*
Burnside, John 261
Burton, James 191
Burton, Richard Francis 79-95 *passim*
Callistratus 97-146 *passim*
Campbell, Roy 241
Carpenter, Edward 258
Carrington, Dora 244-247
Casement, Roger 209
Cassander 97-146 *passim*
Chaeronea, The Order of 97-146 *passim*
Churchill, Winston 224, 227
Cirrha 25-35 *passim*
Cleitus 97-146 *passim*
Clement V 17
Clement VII 24
Cleombrotus 97-146 *passim*
Cleopatra 79-95 *passim*
Cleveland Street Telegram Scandal 195-200
Companion Cavalry 97-146 *passim*
Cory, Johnson 208
Cowboys 256
Croesus 25-35 *passim*
Cumberland, Duke of 195
Currey, Henry 63-65 *passim*
Damian, Cardinal of Ostia 13
Darius III 97-146 *passim*

Freemasons 15, 23-26
Freud, Sigmund 205
Frey, Roger 211, 240
Gallienne, Richard Le 40
Garnett, David 228-248 *passim*
Gaulle, Charles de 204
Gedrosian Desert 97-146 *passim*
Geer, Will 260
Gerber, Henry 250-252
Gernreich, Rudi 253-271 *passim*
Gertler, Mark 247
Goldsworthy, Godsworthy Lowes 210
Gordon, Charles 65-78 *passim*
Got, Bernard de 16
Graff, Anton 49-63 *passim*
Graham, Robert 63-65 *passim*
Grand Orient de France 24
Grant, Angelica 228-248 *passim*
Grant, Duncan 35, 214, 228-248 *passim*
Grant, James 79-95 *passim*
Great Schism 18
Greek View of Life, The 211
Griffith Park 262
Gruber, James 254
Hades 25-35 *passim*
Hallam, Arthur 205-206
Hammond, Charles 197-198
Hampshire, HMS 65-78 *passim*

Napier, Charles 79-95 *passim*
Nemean Games 97-146 *passim*
Newgate Prison 194
Newton, Arthur 198
Nicholson, John 97-146 *passim*
Nicomachus 97-146 *passim*
Noel, Roden 216
Nogaret, Guillaume de 17
Olympic Games 97-146 *passim*
ONE 256
Orange Free State 65-78 *passim*
Order of Chaeronea 97-146 *passim*
Outremer 8, 12
Ovid 25-35 *passim*
Pammenes 97-146 *passim*
Panathenaea Games 97-146 *passim*
Parmenion 97-146 *passim*
Parnassus, Mount 25-35 *passim*
Parnell, Kenneth 265
Partridge, Ralph 244-247
Parysatis 97-146 *passim*
Passage to India, A 248
Pausanias 97-146 *passim*
Payens, Hugues de 11
Pearce, Joseph 37
Pelopidas 97-146 *passim*
Peloponnesian Wars 97-146 *passim*
Perdicas II 97-146 *passim*

Raffalovich, Marc-André 41
Read, Piers Paul 215
Reuter 65-78 *passim*
Rhodes, Cecil 63-65 *passim*
Richards, Ben 221
Richmond, George 217
Rievaulx, Aelred de 10
Roche, Paul 228-248 *passim*
Romance of a Choir-Boy 97-146 *passim*
Room with a View, A 248
Rosebery, Archibald Primrose 46
Ross, Robert 38-39
Rossbach, Battle of 49-63 *passim*
Rothschild, Victor 204
Rowland, Chuck 253-271 *passim*
Roxana 97-146 *passim*
Royal Geographical Society 79-95 *passim*
Russell, Bertrand 220
Sacred Band 97-146 *passim*
Sade, Marquis de 97-146 *passim*
Saladin 14
Salamis, Battle of 97-146 *passim*
Salomé 44
Satyrus 97-146 *passim*
Scented Garden, The 79-95 *passim*
Schuinshoogte 65-78 *passim*
Schwabe, Maurice 191
Seven Years' War 49-63 *passim*

[My autobiography *Michael Hone His World, His Loves*]

Made in United States
North Haven, CT
21 October 2022